DOTS:
Developing Others Through Service

Starting with ME!

By: Nathaniel Woods, Jr

ISBN: 978-0-578-72608-3

Dedication:

This resource is dedicated to my four heroes who have challenged me to live in love:

Linda Knight (mom), PageCarol Woods (wife), Nate Woods III (son), and Angelo Woods (son).

Table of Contents

WORKBOOK

INTRODUCTION

This book is for individuals who have dreams and have yet to wake up and create the reality they desire. This book is also for the individual who's started moving toward their end goal but somehow stopped making forward progress. Keep this in mind as you read through each section of the book.

This resource was intended to be read with the companion workbook. As you read through the book use the workbook to capture your thoughts, ideas, questions, timelines, frustrations, milestones, and more. Use the companion workbook to journal your process and to capture your answers to the questions that I ask you after you complete each chapter. You will get more out of the reading if you and a friend, business partner, colleague, mentee, etc. each get the book and create some dialogue around each chapter as you read through it.

Hopefully, whoever that individual is will provide another vantage point and challenge your perspective to help pull the best out of you. The book is structured with 4 sections that introduces an idea with a phrase. Within each section will be 3-4 chapters diving into those ideas. At the end of each section is a biblical perspective. A chapter that ties faith to what I'm writing about. This is a way that I honor my faith and inform others that the majority of serving others, starting with yourself, runs parallel with faith. Whether you share the same faith as me or not, it will challenge you because much of those chapters challenge your behaviors as it relates to leading/serving yourself and others.

One time, someone asked me about my success (which I believe is a word best defined through personal perspective). First, I gave credit to the grace of God; and, second, I gave myself credit for waking up from the dream state I was in.

This takes me back to the time before I pursued my Master's Degree. I thought about getting my Master's Degree. I dreamt about it, I talked about it, I even journaled it. I thought about it so much that when it was time to register for classes, I couldn't stop thinking about it. I thought about how difficult it would be to juggle my classes with having a wife, a newborn, a full-time job, and serving as a Pastor. I thought about the situation so much that the enrollment and registration period for that year had come and gone.

Man, another missed opportunity!

I was extremely upset that I missed the registration deadline because I wanted to get my Masters' Degree, which would allow me to pursue the things in life that were important to me. I didn't let it get me down for too long because I began to think through the process again. Before I realized it, three years passed, and I never attempted to apply for my Master's Degree, but I thought about it! I was considering all the variables...or at least that's what I would tell myself.

After the third year passed, I remembered a quote I heard from this man on TV named Dr. Myles Monroe.

"The wealthiest place in the world," Dr. Monroe declared, "is not the gold mines of South America or the oil fields of Iraq or Iran. They are not the diamond mines of South Africa or the banks of the world. The wealthiest place on the planet is just down the road. It is the cemetery. There lie buried companies that were never started, inventions that were never made, bestselling books that were never written, and masterpieces that were never painted. In the cemetery is buried the greatest treasure of untapped potential. Don't go to the grave with your treasure still in you!"

Most people never wake up out of their dream state. They grow old and give up on their dreams just to leave this life never fulfilling or even attempting to accomplish their dreams. That is the statement that challenged me to make a conscious decision to wake up and apply for school the following year.

Candidly speaking, I put away my fears! I was afraid to wake up because I was fearful of success. I was afraid of attending school and completing that goal. I was afraid because I never gave thought to what I would do next. I was afraid because I didn't have anyone to model this part of my life after.

Many of you are in the same spot I was in or can relate to this story from my life. Fear has prevented many people from moving forward in life. Some of you are reading this opening section and you're saying to yourself, "I have a J-O-B. I'm making some money – I'm doing ok!" Keep in mind, this resource isn't about you accomplishing someone else's dream. This resource is to help you accomplish your goals.

You can accomplish your personal goals while working a job or having a career. Wake up from the dream, write down what you want to do, create a plan, and take action. This book will help you identify behaviors to recognize you're still in a dream state concerning your goals and leadership. You will learn how to wake up and put your thoughts into an action plan to start moving toward your end goal. Take some time to answer the questions in the workbook before proceeding to the next section.

PART I

I Had A Dream!

(No, You're Still Sleeping)

CHAPTER 1

EVENTUALLY, YOU MUST WAKE UP!

I'm young and running for my life. No matter where I go and hide, he continues to follow me. It's as if I have a scent he's able to pick up and locate my whereabouts. Who is he?

The murderer that broke into my house. As he was attacking my family, I decided to run for help by jumping out the back window of my house. I was only 11 years old, so running was expected. My house was surrounded by woods – I had to run in the woods so he couldn't find me. As I got further away, he seemed to make his way to me. I waited as he rushed by where I was hiding.

I heard him say, "The kid couldn't have gone far," as he turned back around to where I was.

I laid perfectly still under a fallen tree limb hoping to blend in. I could tell he was frustrated because he stomped on the ground and walked off. Without triggering him to come back, I continued to lie still in hopes that he would flee the scene. I fell asleep from laying so still so long.

I woke up. "Surely I've been under this limb long

enough that the intruder is gone," my inner voice whispered.

As I built up the courage to slide out from under the limb, I looked over to see what I could use to pull myself out.

As I looked to my right, I didn't see anything. As I looked the other way in the dark of the night, I saw the man lying on the ground looking at me!

My body froze over. I cried.

I screamed.

As the perpetrator started approaching me, I woke up...

It was all a dream!

What I just shared was a nightmare I had years ago when I was living in Alexandria, Virginia. The reality is many of you feel like you're in a nightmare right now because you see yourself in a better place. However, reality has you in a bad place.

You know you're greater than your current bank account, but reality keeps you making it check by check.

You know you're not living remotely close to your potential; but, currently, you don't see a way to better yourself.

You will continue to feel this way until you wake up from your dream state. Having a dream about where you want to be is a great thing and will build hope as long as you know you can make it happen. But, when you don't see movement in real life, getting you closer to your dream, different emotions breed. You become anxious and impatient; and, you feel like you're in a nightmare.

Dreaming is simply a way to visualize what you want internally. However, to move forward and bring the dream to reality, you must wake up. The longer you stay in the dream state without forwarding progress, the faster your dream will turn into a nightmare.

As you're dreaming of something greater for yourself, your family, your community, your nation, and your everything, be thankful. It's possible to want, want, want so much you forget to be thankful for what you have.

It's a delicate balance to be content and motivated at the same time.

It is possible!

Throughout this journey, I want to challenge you to be thankful for where you are and use your current situation as the first step in gaining momentum. Please refer to the workbook to answer the questions concerning this chapter.

Wake up! Wake up! Wake up! Now, let's work!

CHAPTER 2

WRITE OUT THE PLAN

Simon Sinek is a world-renowned speaker and published author on leadership. As you're writing out your plan, I encourage you to read Sinek's book Start with Why. In his book, Sinek gives insights into making a move in life and never forgetting why you moved in the first place. Sinek teaches there must be a "why" behind every decision you make. It's critical to know why you're going to college, starting a business, deciding to teach, opening a pop-up boutique, attending medical school, becoming a construction worker, or making any other significant move. What you're building through your move is the vehicle that will get you where you want in life. Your "why" is the fuel for your vehicle. We will get to the vehicle; however, without fuel, the vehicle is pointless.

Let me be clear before we go any further: you can work for someone your entire life and complete your own goals. Not everyone is cut out to be self-employed or a business owner; but, you don't have to quit your day job to fulfill your heart's desires. For some of you reading this book, your place of employment will be the source of income to help you move to greatness – just make sure you have a winning budgeting plan.

Speaking of a plan...

Writing out your plan is a seemingly easy thing to do, especially if you've done it before. Reality check: most people haven't been taught to write out a plan for life... they've only planned for investments and business. Many investment/business plans are written, ignoring the fact that life is an investment and needs planning, too. Occasionally I'll see a plan jam-packed with the "what." The individual has done a great job communicating what they want to do; however, they've often neglected to share the "why" and "how." If the "what" is the vehicle and the "why" is the fuel, then "how" would be the motor and tires of the vehicle. The "how" is the life and blood of writing out the plan.

Think about a pep rally: fans come together, someone delivers a speech to share "why" we're here (we love the team) and "what" we're going to do (we're going to win); but, nobody ever hears the "HOW" (for good reason if you're a coach!). So, being excited to go somewhere and not having a plan of action is merely a pep rally. What is your "how"?

My team and I took a couple of days in a secluded location to focus on and finalize a workshop we were preparing to facilitate across the country. During this team-building process of finalizing the workshop, one of the team members led us in an exercise called the "PB&J Exercise." The purpose of the exercise was to get the team to write out every step of making a peanut butter and jelly sandwich. It was extremely funny to watch one of our facilitators act out the steps the group wrote down as their process of making a PB&J sandwich. It was hilarious because we tend to have a vision of doing something, but we don't take the time to think about every single step it will take to complete it.

Every. Single. Step.

In the "how" phase of writing your plan, you should attempt the PB&J exercise first. Some of you may not need to be as detailed in your plan; however, the more detailed the plan, the easier it will be to execute the plan (especially when you add timelines to each step or action). Each action item is considered a milestone. Milestones are essential for people like me because I am motivated by deadlines. Many times, I spend every waking moment on the need to accomplish a task; and, I sometimes struggle with celebrating the little things along the way. Milestones help us to reach our end goal, and they provide markers to pause and celebrate along the way.

Small successes in succession will lead to overall success.

Often, my wife and my mentors have to remind me to celebrate a particular milestone in my plan.

Set milestones as a reminder to be thankful for where you are without settling for your current position. There's a huge difference between celebrating a milestone and celebrating the accomplishment of reaching your end goal! I have family and friends who celebrate their past milestones so much that they've neglected their future. Every milestone doesn't need to be celebrated with dinner or vacation.

Earlier in the chapter, I mentioned the "what" is the vehicle by which you will get to your end goal. I always start with the "why" and "how" of the vehicle. Once I have a solid response to the "why" and "how" the true "what" is revealed. We all have ideas of things we want to accomplish in life. We don't get traction on these items without considering why we're doing it, how we're going to do it, or if it makes sense to do it at all.

There's a harsh reality we need to examine in this "what" "why" "how" process. If you don't take action by completing the milestones in a reasonable time frame, you're still dreaming. You can't take action and sleep at the same time. Wake up and move toward the goal – then it's called progress.

You can do it!

One more reality to consider: grow at a pace you can handle. This is not to be used as an excuse or an out.

What I'm talking about is managing your time. Time management has three components that you need to know:

1. **Task:** What is it that you need to do? Make a list.

2. **Allotment:** How much time will each item need? How much time in your day do you have to commit to getting the items listed done outside of your prior engagements (work, family time, studying for school, etc.)?

3. **Interruptions:** We get interrupted by life almost always. Give yourself time to flex your schedule or week for interruptions/emergencies.

Each component has everything to do with how you plan. If you're in high school and plan to run for President, you don't start your campaign at eighteen years old. However, you can plan to run by getting involved now, developing a support system now, taking an internship or job in the local government now, and so many other relevant tasks to do...now.

Don't limit yourself to planning for one area in your life at a time. You may need to do this to manage your finances better, develop the rental property, losing/gaining weight, joining an organization, dating, or _____. Don't limit yourself. Also, don't limit yourself to planning on your own. You need an accountability partner along the way. Remaining connected to somebody, or a small group, who will give you candid feedback will be beneficial for you and help you remain balanced. There's not one person on this planet that's made it in life on their own – we all have had some assistance and will always need someone.

Please refer to the workbook to answer the questions concerning this chapter.

CHAPTER 3

GET CONNECTED

Years ago, my mother and I were having a conversation about life. I was a new store manager and doing well at the time. I needed to speak with my mother for advice on how to handle a situation; but, without allowing me to go into too much of the situation, my mother stopped me.

"Son," she said, "you're at a point now where I cannot take you any further. You need to get a mentor – someone who can help you go further than I can take you in this area." I gave my mother the biggest hug and thanked her. Before this conversation, my mom was my mentor! She's still one of my mentors. She is my HERO!

My mother encouraged me to get connected to others, and connecting with others requires an understanding of different types of relationships. Developing healthy, authentic relationships is the most critical thing you can do if you have a desire to grow. The term authentic is defined as "not false or copied; genuine; real." Before we dig into the "why" and "how" of establishing healthy relationships, let's discuss the "what." What types of relationships should you be concerned with? Thomas Dexter Jakes speaks of 3 types of people who have challenged the way I view relationships.

1. **Confidants:** People you can trust and confide in about personal matters and secrets. They're in it for you. They love you, unconditionally. This type of friend will not abandon you in a time of need. Not everyone can be your confidant. There's not but a few of them in your life.

2. **Constituents:** People who are not for you. They are for what you are for. They are for the causes you represent, not you. As long as you are for what they are for they will walk with you. If they ever meet someone who can further them better than you can, they will leave you because they weren't for you in the first place. Don't share your dreams with your constituents because they will desert you and try to fulfill the dream without you.

3. **Comrades:** These people are not for you, nor are they for what you're for. They simply are against what you're against. There's just a common goal for both of you, and that's why they're around you. Once the common cause is gone, so are they. Don't share your dreams with comrades because they won't support it – they were never for you in the first place.

People typically don't have 3 or 4 confidants in a lifetime because it takes a lot of time and energy to develop and maintain someone at this level of relationship.

Many of us have a large number of constituents.

Constituents are around you to accomplish a goal. The goal means more to them than the relationship with you. This is similar to people you work with: you never knew them before you started working there; then, once you're working together, you become close. If you or they leave the workplace, the relationship dissolves (obviously there are anomalies).

TD Jakes said it best, "Constituents are like scaffolding. They're close to you like scaffolding to a building. Once the building is completely built, the scaffolding comes down and goes away." Constituents are like this in your workplace and your life. I have a few people I share my dreams with because they will keep me on pace and challenge me to grow. I can confide in them, and they can confide in me. Comrades are individuals who dislike you in private and smile as they walk beside you in public. This is the type of person who appears as a friend but doesn't have your best interest in mind.

You mustn't lose perspective. The same way you're categorizing people you know into one of these three categories right now in your head (and, I know you are!), you fall into one of the three categories for other people when they look at you! Being balanced is knowing you play both roles in life. Categorizing people or being categorized is just the way it is; it isn't evil, it's balance. Again, I want you to think about which role you play in your relationships.

I'm shooting from the hip now. For you to impact your community by leading where there are deficiencies, you must recognize a critical point. You must be willing to establish relationships with people who don't believe what you believe, look like you, vote like you, or even want what you want in life. You must become a person who is able to have a conversation with anyone. You have to get out of the box of what's normal to you.

The type of relationship I love the most is the mentor relationship. A mentor is an experienced and trusted advisor. Mentors will celebrate with you; however, they're not overly impressed by your accomplishments. Mentors will encourage you; but, they'll also have candid conversations with you to keep you grounded. This is an essential relationship, if not one of the most valuable relationships.

One of my first mentors is Mr. Rick. In fact, he's still one of my mentors! As my family started our family business, Mr. Rick mentored me. We would meet occasionally and talk on the phone about how to run a business and how to encourage my team and drive results. I appreciate you, sir!

I have mentors in *each area* of my life. You should have someone in every important area of your life to mentor you. The same way a business owner would have a Chief Officer or Leader of each department of the business, you need a Leader in every area of your life. You need mentorship in your finances, health, spirituality, relational, and so on.

As you learn more about these areas in your life, you have a duty and responsibility to share what you've learned with someone else to help them the same way someone helped you. Some would say pay it forward; however, I say treat others the same way you want to be treated. If you develop others in areas where you're strong, someone will see your heart of serving, and they will serve you.

You do not become a person's mentor because you've shared one or two pointers in life. You become someone's mentor when they ask you to be a mentor, or they mention you as a mentor to others and ask for your leadership. You don't have the right to title yourself someone's mentor unless it's been mutually agreed upon. As a mentor, share with the individual what you see in them and what has attracted you to them. Let them know what you can offer in the relationship and what you would like out of it.

Also, just because you're the boss doesn't make you the mentor. When you're the boss, the team follows you because they have to. Leadership means that the team follows you, in part, because they trust you; and, this happens after or during a relationship-building process. Everything moving forward will be based on relationships. As you start to establish critical relationships in life, don't build false relationships. Be transparent and truthful...be authentic. The reality is most of the time you cannot offer much in relationships except the most valuable piece... being a solid friend! I can't provide my mentors as much as they're offering me; however, I can (and do) provide candid feedback. I don't idolize them, which they respect more than anything. Here's my leadership statement: "Worthwhile conversations will bring about worthwhile relationships. Worthwhile relationships will give you access. Access allows you influence." You have access to the companion workbook, don't forget to utilize the tool.

CHAPTER 4

BIBLICAL PERSPECTIVE

As the Israelites progressed in a relationship toward God, the High Priests were instructed to write out the visions they had and to make it plain. This is everything I described earlier in this book.

The context in which I grew up, I didn't see spiritual people with business acumen. The people I saw were gung-ho about their relationship with God; however, they struggled to obtain an education, budgeting their money, or progressing in the community. I could see this, even at an early age. I couldn't understand the lack of being balanced in life. I was young, so I made the wrong comments because I didn't realize how to ask the right questions, offer suggestions, or lead by example. I pray my family and friends can/will forgive me for my ignorant remarks when I was young. As I've grown, in age and perspective, I've learned how to communicate my questions better. From that, I've learned about and understood much of what I saw when I was younger.

Let's dive into three areas of the Holy Bible that I live by and use in my leadership approach.

Area 1: Doers, not hearers only. James 1: 22 says, "But be doers of the word, and not hearers only, deceiving yourselves." Keeping in context, the scripture is speaking about your relationship with Christ and what it looks like.

Essentially, James is saying, "Brothers and sisters, don't just talk about how we should live as believers of Christ, but show it." If you're not a believer in Jesus Christ – this still applies to you. Don't be a person who talks about everything without walking it out. Our credibility in life comes not only when we talk about what we know, but when we apply what we know. Have you started applying yourself to the things that matter to you? Are you talking about your dreams and going back to sleep, or are you talking about it and making progress towards it?

The last part of that scripture says, "deceiving yourselves." I know people who struggle with completing whatever task is in front of them. They start everything strong, and they even start well. They get midway through whatever they started, then they stop because they lose sight of the end goal. Then the talking begins... they talk so much they trick themselves into thinking they're making progress by planning their next move. The reality is they're just talking and not preparing the next move; but, to them, they're planning. I was once this exact way. If you find yourself in a place similar to this, you must stop talking and start doing. You're lying to yourself saying you're going to do and you haven't moved forward in 3 days, 3 weeks, 3 months, 3 years, 3 decades, and so on. Stop deceiving yourself.

Area 2: Write the vision and make it plain. Habakkuk 2:2-3 says, "Then the LORD answered me and said, 'Write the vision and make it plain on tablets, that he may run who reads it.'" A lesson I teach my team is that the more you move up, the more you have to shut up. This isn't me being disrespectful – this is me informing my team that they will hear things the higher up they move.

This is also true when you have a vision and want to bring the dream to life. One sign of a great leader is they know how to keep their mouth closed and not talk too much. This was particularly difficult for me at the beginning of my career because I was prideful and a bit arrogant. I wanted people to know I knew a bit more than they did, and I wanted people to see I had a position (a title). Desiring notoriety caused me to compromise the discretion that was needed to move to the next level, so I didn't move. I talked about my ideas too much. I saw someone else moving with one of my ideas.

That hurt!

But, I spoke too much and didn't write out a plan of action with some dates and follow-ups. Someone else had enough sense to write out an action plan and move on it. So my great idea became someone else's retirement plan.

If you get to a place where you're talking too much to too many people, stop yourself and start writing your plan. Or revisit the plan you've already written out, and you might find you have some tweaks to make. Or, just stop talking (shut up).

I have a vision for every area of my life the same way I have a mentor for every area of my life. Have you documented your vision in addition to a plan for your team members to execute? Habakkuk instructed the people to write the vision and make it plain. Those are directives; and, directives are to be followed – not negotiated. It's important to know this because God will bless what you desire to do in life. However, you must work at it. It's more than praying and God doing all the work. It's more like this: pray, God provides you the grace to do the work, and you work toward the goal. Success!

Area 3: Learn leadership through followership. Ruth and Naomi are examples of this area. Read through Ruth 1: 6-18. Being connected to the best person available is always the best thing if you desire to grow in a particular area. I continue to remain around people who have completed what I'm working towards, especially those who are leaders so I can continue to learn how to lead by following. Not only am I putting myself in place to be a student of others, but I'm also making myself available for the next group of individuals that see me as a mentor/leader.

Ruth lost everything, and instead of going back home, she stayed connected to Naomi and allowed Naomi to mentor her. Under the leadership and guidance of

Naomi, Ruth was able to strategically position herself for success according to the times. One of my good friends often says, "I don't care about how many people you're leading. I'm more impressed by seeing you're led by someone (accountability)." Ruth listened to Naomi's advice. The followership method put Ruth in a great place in life, and Naomi reaped greatly in the process. Don't let the opportunity pass without answering the questions for this chapter in the workbook.

Who will you stay connected to?

<u>PART II</u>

Reminder: This resource is for the individual who has dreams and has yet to wake up and create their desired reality. This resource is also for the individual who's started moving toward their end goal but somehow stopped making forward progress.

CHAPTER 5

SONIC BOOM

A sonic boom is considered a shock wave that is produced by an aircraft or other object flying at a speed equal to or exceeding the speed of sound and is heard on the ground like a clap of thunder. A sonic boom only happens when an object is making forward progress at a rapid speed. The people you have around you consistently act as a mirror. If the people you keep the closest to you are not moving forward, you're probably not moving forward either. In the vehicle of life, when everyone around you is in park and you are, too, everyone is okay with being in park with you. However, the moment you shift out of park into drive (making forward progress), it's a sign to everyone else that they're in park and not moving. Your movement will either rally others to move along with you, or you will be ostracized (hated on) by others for moving. Think back to Ruth and Naomi, then think about who you are surrounding yourself with.

Let the haters hate because *your* forward progress is extremely necessary!

There are three points I want to share with you about movement: obstacles, maneuvering, and weight. These points aren't meant to scare you away, they're just reminders about how forward movement.

POINT 1: OBSTACLES

As you gain momentum, you'll recognize obstacles aren't as difficult to break through as you might've thought when you were at a standstill. Additionally, you'll realize many situations will work themselves out without you having to stop moving. Forward progress builds momentum, which is a powerful tool. John Maxwell said, "If a train is moving full speed ahead and there is a concrete barrier in front of it, it will smash through the barrier without any problem. However, if that same train is at a standstill and you put two small bricks in front of the wheels, it will not move." The train is only powerful when it has momentum. The same is true in life and with your forward movement.

POINT 2: MANEUVERING

My wife and I went jet skiing with some good friends.

As we were out on the water, I realized I couldn't turn this machine unless I was moving forward. The same principle applies when driving a car. It's only possible to maneuver a vehicle when it's in motion. Leading a team and a family requires forward movement to maneuver properly. You can cover more ground by moving forward and making adjustments as you go rather than stopping every time. Movement is necessary before you make a turn or adjust the direction you're going in; therefore, movement makes maneuvering possible.

POINT 3: WEIGHT

The weight of the cargo you're carrying will determine how far out you need to plan before making any adjustments. The lighter and smaller the cargo, the more reactive and impulsive you can be. The heavier and larger the cargo, the more you need to plan and strategize before making any adjustments. When a Volkswagen Beetle approaches a stop sign and needs to stop quickly, the driver can slam on the brakes, and the beetle will stop almost immediately; however, if an 18-wheeler did the same thing carrying a heavy load, it wouldn't be able to stop as the Beetle did. If the 18-wheeler attempted a sudden stop, there's a high risk that the truck would run through the stop sign causing a collision or the brakes would lock up causing the 18-wheeler to jackknife and potentially create other catastrophes. No matter the outcome, someone could get hurt, and the driver could damage the vehicle or the load being hauled. To prevent jackknifing, you must be aware of the weight you're carrying. Weight is being used metaphorically to symbolize deadlines, the pressure at work, the pressure at home, agendas, daily responsibilities, the people you're responsible for, bills, life, and so you can plan for any adjustments.

Will you know every adjustment that needs to be made?

No!

So, create a plan for emergency stops or sudden turns and how to handle them.

Review these three points: obstacles, maneuvering, and weight. For forward progress to continue, you must know where you are: what obstacles you face, movement leads to maneuvering, and the weight you're carrying. Knowing where you are requires you to be brutally honest with yourself. For most individuals, admitting they're not where they want to be is difficult. Keep in mind it's easier to say you're not where you want to be when you have a plan to get to where you want to go. No matter where you are, you must be able to admit where you are in life, work, or leadership to move forward.

Once you admit where you are you can go back to the Introduction of this book, "I had a Dream," and construct a plan to keep or start moving forward. Please refer to the workbook to answer the questions concerning this chapter.

All movement isn't progress, so be sure you're moving forward!

CHAPTER 6

MOTION ISN'T PROGRESS
(RECOGNIZE WHERE YOU ARE)

I remember sitting on an airplane flying from North Carolina to Florida because I was transferred as a District Manager to help grow the market. While on the airplane, I looked over and started speaking to a gentleman while his wife was asleep.

I said, "Hey! How are you doing? My name is Nate."

A simple introduction, and all of a sudden, he starts to tell me about his life, who he is, and where he comes from. I was intrigued!

He looks at my wedding band and says, "Young man, how long have you been married?"

At the time, I'd been married seven years. "Seven years. We have two boys and are excited about marriage. We're still honeymooning!" I said. We laughed for a moment. I asked him how many years he'd been married.

He said, "Young man I've been married for 42 years, and I've loved every part of it! It's fun, it's sad, it's easy, it's hard; but, I'm hers, she's mine, and we love each other deeply."

I applauded him. Literally!

After hearing he had been married 42 years, and taking in his commentary about marriage, I just started clapping – a soft clap – but, I clapped to let him know that I was congratulating him on such a huge accomplishment. You do not hear things of that sort nowadays – that wasn't just good, it was great!

Seven months later, I met a couple who walked into one of my work locations.

I greeted them, "Hello! Welcome to the store. My name is Nate, and your name, please?"

They responded.

"What brings you in today?" I asked.

I wanted to connect with the guests, so we began a conversation. I noticed they had a different accent than those who lived in our local area; so, I asked them where they were from. He told me where they were from.

I asked the gentleman, "Is this your wife?" He replied, "Yeah, this is my wife."

She frowned. Huh?!

I asked how long they had been married, and he said they had been married forty-something years. Just as before, I did my clap and congratulated the couple.

The gentleman's wife said, "It is nothing to celebrate; the fact that we remained married is not why you should clap because we are not happy together."

Wow! That's not great. Is it even good?

That hit me in the chest and made me think. Generally, we associate being married or sticking it out with success. That's not success! If you are in it and you are miserable the entire time you're in it, that's not success. Just like marriage, long- term career or job success isn't based on longevity alone. Just because you kept a job for 12 years does not mean you are successful. Just because you've owned a business for 16 years does not mean you are successful. What if your business put you in debt and you had to work another job all 16 years just to break even, is that success? Operating your business and working another job to support your business – is that what you originally intended to do or want to be known by?

Listen to the question I ask myself regularly, "Is someone else being positively impacted by you functioning in your role?" Or does everyone say, "Nate's just here, he's my boss? He's been here for 16 years, and everything's the same – nothing gets accomplished or ever changes." What good is it for us to be excited about something and we do it year after year after year after year, and we regret it, we hate it, we despise it, it doesn't grow, and the people involved don't grow either?

I want to challenge you to think about who you are as a leader: look at yourself first, then others. Think about your level of self-discipline, commitment to the grind, and ability to educate yourself. How can you challenge your team/mentee/associates to do the things necessary to move from good to great when you don't do those things yourself? How can you talk about self-development when you're not looking at how to be a better spouse/parent/follower/leader? What's your purpose as a leader, and are you fulfilling that purpose daily?

The point of the story of the two married couples is *motion isn't progress*. Countless couples stay together for years and say, "We make it work," but never make progress in their marriage. Some never challenge each other to grow emotionally, never support each other's dreams, never enjoy each day as it comes with each other, but complain about each other's actions. Marriage becomes a dead-end job as opposed to a healthy and thriving relationship that makes everyone around the relationship better people.

Now the marriage is focused on the children, so the parents don't have to spend time addressing each other. The only time they talk is when it concerns the children. What lesson does that teach the children, "fake it until you make it"? At work it's the same thing, you'll find yourself doing what you hate in life just to pay the bills. Then, you realize, "I've spent the last 25 years of my life chasing money, but I don't enjoy what I'm doing; and, it's making life miserable for everyone around me." There's motion, but no progress... much like a merry-go-round.

Often times we're in similar situations in all areas of

life: we're working and moving around, but there's no progress. If you've ever managed a group, business, staff, church group, property, and so on, you would see it more. Sometimes you'll see yourself doing busywork, but at the end of the day when you assess what you've accomplished that day, you learn you didn't complete anything that was of significance. This is motion without progress.

Here's my Starter Kit to self-discipline to ensure you're moving in the right direction and continuing to do so:

- Start Early: When you start early, you can commit to your personal things first. I do my bible study and workout in the mornings. I've learned that when I take care of me first, I'm better for everyone around me. If you can't add time to the end of the day, you must take from the time in the morning. Start your day by investing in yourself in some form or fashion. Almost 85% of this book was written between 6:30am and 7:35am every morning. Start the day investing in you, and you'll provide a better response at work because you're not neglecting your vision. A dietician once told me, "What you start your day eating is what you will crave for the rest of your day." At the time, I was taking in a lot of sugar. I learned over time to acquire an appetite to live, no matter the cost.

Now I don't eat to satisfy my taste buds every day. I love the taste of living a healthy life so drinking water, eating vegetables, exercising, turning down sugars, spending quality time with my family, and waking up early taste good to me. I had to change what I started my day with, and that determined how I felt the rest of the day. When I work out in the mornings, I'm always full of energy and ready to get after the day. When I used to sleep in, I felt sluggish – the entire day was slow for me. It's all mental; however, if we don't change the way we think, our bodies will continue to do the same thing. Change the way you start your day, and it will change your entire day.

- To-Do List: Everything you need to complete or do today should be written down on a list, including going to lunch. Spend your day completing that checklist according to which items are time-sensitive (must be done by a certain time) and which items will provide you the most significant ROI (Return on Investment). Lunch is important – it's your time to disconnect from what you've been working on to clear your mind. Lunch is a short reset. Some days you will not complete your to-do list. A part of ending your day should include writing out the to-do list for the next day and put those items you didn't complete today on the top of the list for tomorrow. If you have to call someone back on your to-do-list, complete that call before you end your day. This brings you a great deal of credibility. As you cross items off your to-do-list, there's a sense of accomplishment. Mentally, you're winning every time you shorten the list. The more you follow this best practice, the less you'll find yourself doing busy work (moving and getting nowhere).

- Communication Strategy: Use a calendar to schedule your appointments. If you have appointments with another person, send them a calendar invite. I heard someone say, "The ink of the mind fades rapidly over time." We cannot remember everything ever discussed in conversation. Keep a notebook/tablet with you to journal and take notes in. It's a great habit, and I see great leaders all over the world doing this exact behavior. This keeps your information fresh and correct (as long as you're taking good notes). It also frees your mind. Albert Einstein said, "Never memorize something that you can look up." Make sure you follow up all phone conversations and meetings with an email summarizing what was discussed. A follow-up means, "I valued our conversation so much that I took time to think about what you said and wanted to schedule another time or give you the points I've gathered." Organizations have to set up systems and processes to make sure the follow up happens. If you understand the value of a follow-up from a leader's perspective, you'll be years ahead of the competition. In any leadership role, you'll hear the word "accountable." The conversation normally goes, "We need to hold our people accountable." The word "accountable" is ignorantly used as if the first responsibility is on the staff; yet, the truth is that the first and second responsibilities are on the leader. The leader should set the expectation (cast vision and explain how to make it a reality) and follow up on the action plan to make sure it's being done. Those are the first and second steps to any growth. The third step would be that the staff is completing the task asked of them or ask for assistance if there's some confusion.

There's a truth most people in business don't discuss: it is possible to be the bad leader of a great team that functions at a high level. I've seen groups naturally perform at a high level no matter who their leader was. The difference was a great leader stepped in and challenged the team not to miss "GREATNESS" because they've settled for "GOOD." When a leader comes in and challenges you to be great, it will draw another type of functioning and performance out of you.

Awesome leaders will challenge your perspective and fuel the fire inside. I believe YOU can draw greatness out of others.

The Sixth President, John Quincy Adams, said this concerning leadership, "If your actions inspire others to dream more, learn more, do more, and become more, you are a leader."

Titles need leaders; leaders don't need a title! First, you have to recognize the greatness in you. It's the duty and obligation of your mentors to help draw it out of you. Your boss/ manager may not know how to pull more out of you.

Naturally functioning at a high-level and not pushing yourself or your teams to get better is "motion without progress." Please refer to the workbook to answer the questions concerning this chapter.

Don't miss GREATNESS because you settled for what was good!

CHAPTER 7

THE ONLY COMPETITION IS YOU

It's 90 degrees outside, blazing hot, the sun is piercing our skin, any hats or shades that could be worn just weren't enough. It is too hot; it is entirely too hot!

Family members are all around laughing, joking, playing, and reminiscing. Outside the house, I look around and see the children running around and playing. IT'S A REUNION! It's a family reunion, and it's an amazing family reunion!

I look to the left and see my grandmother sitting down, and family is all around talking and laughing. I look out and see my uncles frying fish. I see all the family members coming in and bringing in different items. My mother whispers into her children's ears, "start breaking down only where everyone is finished eating." At the end of it all, family members are leaving to go home. I thought to myself, "They get in, spend quality time with everyone, and go home."

Throughout the entire day, we had different

assignments. I can't speak for any other family member; I can only speak for what my mother told hers. She taught us to serve through serving our family members. The more and more she embraced the idea of serving others, the more we served. No matter what event or function was presented, my mother would take the opportunity to cook. Along with cooking came serving, and along with serving came cleaning, and it used to bother me for years. I used to say, "Mom, why are we cleaning all the time? When everyone else was laughing, having a good time, and enjoying one another, we were serving." It was upsetting for a while; but, God orchestrated a plan through my mother to teach us how to serve others no matter who they were. I learned how to serve others, not how to be served.

My mother's push to serve our family and friends was the springboard for me. That has been my approach to everything I have done up to this point – this servanthood – helping and being excited about helping. At first, I didn't like it nor did I understand it. I didn't know what it meant to serve others. I didn't see the value of being selfless nor did I know the value it would have on people if I did it with joy in my heart. I didn't care to serve because I always saw others being served, so I wanted to be served.

By the time I'd become an adult with a family of my own, my mission was to help others however I could. I moved to Florida due to work, and I got connected with a church, Orlando World Outreach Center with Pastor Tim Johnson.

Through the leadership of Pastor Tim and the church staff, a culture of serving has been developed in this church. I didn't know anything about serving at this level. I always spoke of serving your way into leadership; but, I was learning something different about serving I didn't fully understand. For a person like me, who was accustomed to speaking all the time and preaching, teaching, doing lecture series, counseling couples, and being involved in the community, I knew what it meant to serve. In Orlando, I was in an unfamiliar place in my life. I didn't know anyone else in my area, I was learning something new in business, but was learning something different about serving I never knew before. My occupation is the thing that brought me to Florida, but my vocation is the thing I was supposed to grow in while being in Florida. That growth has proven to feed back into my occupation, making it greater; and, that is servanthood.

I was excited I met this Pastor Tim Johnson, an amazing guy! When I got there initially, I wanted to identify what I could fix, so everyone would know what I could bring to the table. As I started talking, I was in the conversation for about 30 minutes, then I realized, I'm having an "OLD" conversation in a "NEW" place. I recognized if I did the same thing or had the same conversation as I did in my past in this new place I would get the same outcome. What I learned at

Orlando World Outreach Center was if you have the heart to serve, then serve where there is a need. No matter if the need feels good or not, no matter if the need brings recognition or not, we should serve.

Serving others is more than bringing food to a table for someone to eat or seating a group of people at a table. Serving is providing a service without looking for any wages, and this is the definition of a bondservant. Service could be imparting some wisdom into someone without expecting anything in return, helping someone in your department by mentoring them, offering an encouraging word to someone who needs it, buying lunch for the person behind you in line, taking time to help a younger student in an area of your strength in school, serving the less fortunate, and many other actions.

I'm going to take this time to be candid. One area I struggled with was comparing myself to others. I'm sure most people can relate to my struggle. Our society is structured in such a way that we feel better or worse in life based on how we rank ourselves against others. I've lived 35 years comparing myself to others. Lecrae, a fantastic artist (in my opinion), said, "If you live by their acceptance, you'll die by their rejection." What a profound statement!

By the way, who are "they?" Your best competitor will always be you. If we took more time to become a better "us," we'd have fewer insecure people walking around. The real question is, "Are you comfortable in your skin?" If you are, is it based on your comparison to other people that you're better than? If you're not, is it based on you comparing yourself to others, and you feel like the lesser of the two? This book wasn't intended for you to beat out the competition, but to beat your very best every day. As you outdo yourself, you'll naturally set yourself apart. You and I both can do greater things in life when we become content in our own skin.

Content doesn't mean complacent. Content is, "I'm good being me; I don't need someone else's name on me (name branded clothes or association with someone) to give me my worth. Insecure people find their worth in wearing someone else's name or have a relationship with someone famous.

Knowing someone wealthy or famous will never change your net worth or value. I don't need to be associated with a particular group of people to define me. I'm not better or less than you. I'm me." You may not fit in with everyone or act like everyone, but that's okay. The exceptionally skilled individuals in life are those who are disciplined enough to work at being a better version of themselves.

Be you, and serve others by teaching them the same.

As my son and I watched a television show together, a commercial came on; and, the commercial featured Lebron James speaking along with other great athletes. They all said the same phrase, "We don't need another (they inserted their name...)!" That's a fact! We don't need another one of them or another me. The world is waiting for YOU! We need your vision, your talents, your skills, your wisdom, and your leadership. As part of your preparation to share your gift with the world, complete the portion in the workbook that speaks to this chapter.

Be *you*!

CHAPTER 8

THE STEPS

Years ago, as a District Manager, I took my team of store managers out for a team-building activity. I wanted the team to grow a little closer by spending time together and sharing new concepts and best practices. Once we arrived at the business, we had to get from the foyer to the main part of the venue by using the stairs. There were 20-30 steps before we could get out of the foyer into the main gaming area where the fun was. Before my team walked up the stairs, I made them stand back, and we watched people go up and down the stairs. In watching people go up and down the stairs we saw people hold onto the rail and go up the stairs one step at a time and I saw people come down the same way. We also witnessed a couple of younger people skipping over steps, two and three at a time, and one person did four! After about five or six minutes passed, someone was going up the stairs and skipping steps until they missed a step they were trying to get on. They slipped and fell forward (their pride was hurt more than they were physically). They banged up their shin.

I looked at my team and asked, "Why do you think that happened?"

My team looked at me and said, "Because they were skipping steps."

I said, "Watch what happens next."

Once the person got up, they walked up the rest of the stairs one step at a time. My team kind of chuckled, they laughed at the concept. What I wanted them to understand, and what I want you to understand is there are many times in life that we try to skip the steps of life. We try to get somewhere extra fast; when we get what we got extra fast we don't appreciate it, we waste it, and we don't take care of it appropriately. We don't know how to maintain it because we skipped the steps, the learning process, in an attempt to get to the finish line.

There is a lesson to be learned on every step we take. That's true in life, especially in leadership. Everything you go through in your journey as a human being is a learning experience – each step taken with your family, with your children, with your significant other, with your career, with the people you lead, and with yourself. We try to hasten the process and get to the end as fast as we can; but, the end result is only appreciated and valued more as you learn along the way. What are you taking from the steps of your life? Each step is significantly important all by itself. Every step provides what the others don't; a specific lesson. It's best to think of every area in life, from the most significant thing down to the simplest thing as a step.

Take a look at Figure 1.1. In this figure, you see "rise" and "tread." The "rise" in life would be the knowledge (information) we obtain. There are many ways to learn information (school, reading, life experience, observations, etc.). If you don't know about a subject or an area of life, you're considered ignorant of that subject or area. To have information and not act on it is considered foolishness.

Wisdom is the application of information according to the Webster dictionary. I'm sure you know of someone who knows a lot of information but refuses to apply it. I do! I don't want to be the person who's taking in information all my life and never utilizing it. That leads me to the "tread," which is the period of application (applying what you've learned in the "rise"). In the definition of the tread, it speaks to the depth of the step. With the application of information comes depth.

Without the application, you're considered shallow.

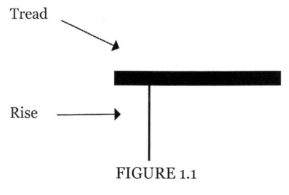

Tread

Rise

FIGURE 1.1

We need both parts of the stairs explained in figure 1.1, and we should live a balanced life of learning and application. I have a few questions for you.

1. What ways are you intentionally learning more?

2. What steps are you taking to apply what you've learned?

3. How will you teach what you've learned to someone else so they can start educating themselves and applying what they've learned?

4. Are you pacing yourself as you're taking the steps of life?

5. What do you need to do periodically to keep you motivated to learn more? (e.g., I need mini vacations/staycations to keep me moving forward each quarter or awards, and certificates motivate me to keep going once or twice a year).

As you walk the stairs of life, do not skip the application to gain knowledge only. Think about spending your time applying the information you don't fully understand. Everything we do we should be balanced. That's in learning, work, marriage, singleness, parenting, and so on. The balance in education is a period of knowledge and a period of application.

In the process of doing both rise and tread – or learning and applying, we gain a valuable tool that you cannot buy in a store...understanding. In all that you get, I urge you to get understanding. The next step is to complete the section in the workbook for this chapter.

Don't stop learning!

CHAPTER 9

BIBLICAL PERSPECTIVE

The Holy Bible speaks of a person who has a form of godliness but denies the power thereof. In other words, it's a person who provides lip service and acts in a way that is different than what they're saying. Their conversation and actions don't match. There are times in our lives where we do that – talk the talk, but don't walk the walk. Instead of illustrating this through my experiences, I'd prefer combining my story with some from the Bible.

After this, you and I both can call out our own areas where we've denied the power of God (Thank God for His amazing grace!). You might be in that place right now in life. I was there before and I still often have to lean on my support group of sisters and brothers in the faith to keep me encouraged now and then. I'm not going over these stories of the faith to give you a reason to have a lapse in your faith and integrity; instead, I'm highlighting a couple greats in the faith so you will see you're not alone.

Abraham (Genesis 20:1-18):

• Abraham lied with the intent to protect his wife. The fear of losing what meant so much to him (his wife), outweighed the faith he had that God would protect his wife. Abraham believed God in other areas of life. However, he struggled in this area (trusting God to protect his wife). This lack of trust in God's protection caused unnecessary issues. In other words, motion and no progress. Abraham only needed to tell the truth and trust that God would deliver him and his wife safely back home.

Peter (Luke 22:54-62)

• Peter followed Jesus and trained under Him daily for years. When Jesus was falsely accused of a crime He didn't commit and was punished to death, Peter followed behind Jesus. While in the crowd he was identified as a Jesus follower, in fear of his life Peter denied Jesus a few times. Peter believed that denying his relationship with Jesus would change the outcome of his life; certain death. Once Peter realized the value of the relationship with Jesus, he was willing to give his life for Jesus.

Recently, I heard a college professor describe this faith race we're in like this, "Jesus ran the race, won it in record time; and, He takes the crown of victory off His head and places it on ours. Then Jesus tells us to take the victory lap. He says, 'I don't care how long it takes, if you fall or not, or if you stumble here and there. Just complete the

61

victory lap.'" As we surrender more of our lives and will over to God, He helps us realize how victorious we are in Him. That doesn't mean we don't have to work or that life will never be hard. We must complete the lap while trusting Him. Oswald Chambers said, "The meaning of prayer is that we get hold of God, not of the answers." We have God, and He's more than enough in all areas of our lives.

Self-Examination: 2 Corinthians 13:5-6 says, "Examine yourselves as to whether you are in the faith. Test yourselves. Do you not know that Jesus Christ is in you? – Unless indeed you are disqualified. But I trust that you will know that we are not disqualified." You can get the most out of your growth by surrounding yourself with people that will give you the truth about your actions. When you start being intentional about your growth you'll get intentional about who you allow in your inner circle. You don't wake up with this mindset. You learn this from watching people, who are great to you, examine themselves; and, they challenge you to examine yourself.

My wife and I decided it was time to get her a new vehicle. We went to the dealership and looked at a few models as we discussed what she really wanted. After we understood what she wanted in a new vehicle, we let the salesperson know. Then, we took a vehicle for a test drive. While driving on a back road, the salesperson asked my wife to slowly act as if she's going to cross into the oncoming lane of traffic. (It was safe to try it out, so she did.) As soon as the car hit the solid line that divided the two lanes, the car immediately started to beep loudly, and the steering wheel auto-corrected and put the vehicle back into the correct lane. So impressed by this auto-correct feature, my wife decided to swerve again.

The vehicle auto-corrected her driving...again!

Self-examination/evaluation is auto-correcting your life. Maybe you're joking too much with your children so they're not taking you seriously when they should. Maybe you're making every excuse under the sun not to commit to completing whatever you start, when in your heart you know you can complete the task. Maybe you're giving your job/church/friends the best of you and giving your spouse your sloppy seconds, even though your spouse deserves your best.

When I was a child in elementary school, firefighters came to the school and taught us what to do if we were on fire. They taught us to stop, drop, and roll. If everyone started doing this just because they wanted to, they'd look crazy because it's not serving a purpose. However, when a person evaluates their current position and realizes they're on fire, they won't look like a fool if they stop, drop, and roll! The fire department provided us with steps to help us examine our situation and act.

Step 1: Stop – stop what you're doing, stop running because the air will feed the fire, stop panicking (you must be as calm as possible to make rational decisions), and stop to evaluate where the fire is on your body.

Step 2: Drop – get to the source that can extinguish the fire (in this case the ground).

Step 3: Roll – roll on the ground to smother the fire between the ground and your body.

You must schedule time to evaluate your progress, so you will know whether or not you're on pace. In the business world, most departments sync up on a weekly call to ensure everyone is in the know, track progress, identify hurdles, course correct, and encourage the team. You can apply this great principle to yourself as a way to evaluate your progress.

The steps of a good man (woman) are ordered: Psalms 37: 23, "The steps of a good man are ordered by the LORD: and he delighteth in his way." After really studying God's Holy Word, I learned that the steps of a righteous man are ordered by the Lord. It is so amazing and comforting to know that God has ordered my steps! Every single step I take, He's divinely ordered and orchestrated it. The steps that I take are not something that is just happening by chance, nor is God aimlessly pointing me in any direction saying, "Whatever happens, happens; and, we'll make the best of it." Nope! He has a plan for my life, and every step I take is getting me closer to fulfilling what He has purposed me for.

Our current generation isn't a fan of the process... and, not because they don't like it. They were introduced to this world with one main concept: you can have it now. We have fast food restaurants that will have your meal in less than 5 minutes. We eat seedless fruit, so we don't go through the process of removing the seeds. We have internet which provides us many conveniences like instant phone calls, emails, pictures, and responses. It's not bad at all. The downside of this convenience is we don't like the process of development – we want the result(s) immediately!

Let's look at how seeds grow. Seeds, like humans, must go through a period of growth. The germination process is similar to the way many people grow. There is a part of brokenness that takes place. We place a seed in the ground with hopes that it will produce. We have to dig a hole, and it is almost like we are burying it. Now the seed goes into a dark place, and many of us as leaders have gone into a dark place. We go through a period of learning which seems to be one of the hardest things because this is the point at which we are trying to find ourselves. We are also trying to find out what God has purposed for us. In the process, we lose a couple of friendships, a couple of relationships change dynamics, and we find ourselves breaking away from some bad habits – maybe even getting away from people who influence us to do the wrong things. This is the germination process, and we find ourselves broken.

If our perspective is right (we hold on to the perspective of Jesus Christ – knowing that He is ordering our steps), then as we are being broken, we must continue to trust Him. We hate the process because it's painful and we don't have all the details. If we hold to the fact that God is ordering our steps, then we have hope (and, the hope is: we won't be here always). Once the Lord gives us the things we need, and once we're able to obtain the things that we're supposed to get out of this, we can move to the next step. As we continue to progress through each step, we find ourselves getting closer to what we're gifted and passionate about. God has given us these steps so that it puts us on a platform. (I'm saying platform, but a platform is merely a place of influence.) When we realize the influence we've been given isn't for us to make a name for ourselves, but rather, make a name for Jesus, we've understood the true purpose.

As we learned previously in this book, so often steps get skipped; and, when the steps get skipped, we miss vital pieces of the lesson. One day, I am going to give my son a car. Currently, he is nine years old, but at age sixteen, the car would be good for him and would work well for him... when he is sixteen and older. Giving him the car now (at age nine!) and putting the keys in his hands, would damage him and others around him. So, I can't give him the car right now. I have to wait and take him through a few vital steps, first. I need to make sure he can make great decisions: know how to drive and know how to budget his money so he can pay for his gas. I need to make sure he is responsible, so I start giving him chores now. Little things, it's the small steps now that are going to amount to the big steps later in his life. I have to start teaching him now to prepare him for the car seven years from now.

As a leader, are you taking your time on the steps? Are you taking time to be developed on every step? Are you charging forward and skipping two and three steps at a time so you can get to your destination faster? When we rush, we believe time is our enemy instead of our ally. If you plan properly and execute what you plan, you'll never have to worry about time being an enemy.

I know you want to get to the result fast (it's a part of our culture), but getting to the destination fast affects people around you. Just because you feel like you are ready, doesn't mean you are. Have you paid attention to how it will affect the people around you when you get on that fourth, fifth, and twentieth step? I can imagine many of you saying, "I'm ready to get promoted." It may require you to travel or relocate to another state. You may be ready, but is your spouse ready?

You may be ready right now, but are your children ready to be without you an additional hour a day? One of the gentlemen I admired once told me, "If your home isn't ready for you to be promoted, you're not ready to be promoted." What a life changing statement! I talk to millionaires regularly who pursued money, and they got it, but now they don't have a family to share it with. I know people who forgot why they started on the path they started on and lost everything pursuing things and forgot what mattered most to them. I know people who've stayed on a step longer and waited for their family; now, they have everything they could ever ask for in life because their family is with them. Spencer Chipping is a friend that chose his family over his career, and he's in a better place now. His choice challenges me to think about if I'm doing what I'm doing for my family or me. It is easy to say I'm making these business decisions to provide for my family. However, if we're candid with ourselves we'll see many times it's not for our family, it for us (our pride, to prove someone wrong, we want a title, we're chasing money, etc.). I appreciate having people around me that value different things in life. Other people I know have watched their team move up the corporate ladder as they moved up (they grew together), and that was their goal – waiting on the step a little longer than others. Every step taken matters!

If you sincerely allow the Lord to order your steps and you consult Him daily, you'll make better steps. Then, you will realize that God works outside of time; and, you will not be deceived by thinking that you're running out of time. The Lord, our God, is ordering everyone's steps... even yours. So keep stepping! Please use the workbook to answer the questions concerning this chapter.

PART III
Rhythm
(In Your Groove)

Reminder: This resource is for the individual who has dreams and has yet to wake up and create their desired reality. This resource is also for the individual who's started moving toward their end goal but somehow stopped making forward progress.

CHAPTER 10

THE MENTAL CHALLENGES OF GROWTH

One morning while driving my children to school, my oldest son said, "Papa, the word on the red and white truck is backwards."

I responded with, "Some things in life appear backwards; but, it's written correctly. The purpose of writing it backwards is so people can read it correctly looking through their side/rearview mirrors."

I angled the mirror so he could see it.

He said, "Oh, I get it. Daddy, it's like writing in code."

I simply laughed.

Reader, I want to show you a code different from the word "ambulance" written on a vehicle. In Figure 2.1, we see a plant. You were probably raised and programmed to think like most of us - we're like a plant. We grow as children in an environment (dirt) where we're nurtured and educated (watered) by external resources. We have leaders and supporters (stem/ roots) to influence us, and we bloom (flower) when all areas work together in concert. The result is the flower gets the opportunity to shine (get light) and help others grow (pollination).

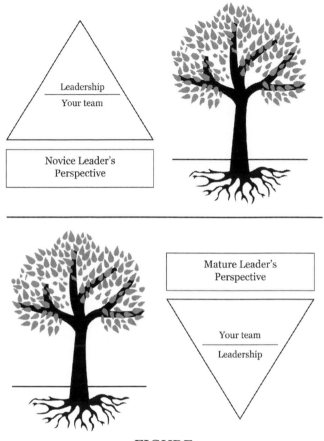

FIGURE 2.1

Candidly speaking, we should rally around our children like the process just described, and they will develop into beautiful flowers. When we're children, we're supposed to be that flower and get that light. When we start to understand the concept of leading ourselves, followership, leadership, parenting, and serving others, that same flower gets turned upside down. As a functioning leader, your responsibility is to become the stem/root so you can feed the people you serve (the flowers) what they need to grow and get as much light as possible. That means the functioning leader must transition from being in the spotlight (flower) to behind the scenes (stem/root) so others can grow. The transition takes time and it can be difficult if we love being in the front.

What would happen if the leader put their time and energy on gathering nutrients (strategizing, coaching, mentoring, and correcting) to feed the flower? We'd have more businesses that operate at the peak of success from a financial and cultural perspective. We'd also see fewer families walking around dysfunctional because the parents would realize they're parents and stop trying to be like, or even liked by, the children. The leaders would be proud to position the children, staff, mentees, and any other constituents to get as much light as possible while still supporting them. The flower would grow more prominent, absorb more light, better feed the roots, and reproduce. If you're leading a group of people, lead them and stop trying to fit in with them. They need leadership more than they need friendship. The same is true for parenting. Look, again, at Figure 2.1 and ask yourself if you are the leaf/flower or the stem/root. Please refer to the workbook to answer the questions concerning this chapter.

Grow to be the stem/root!

CHAPTER 11

I GOT THIS!
(TITLE VS. FUNCTION)

Experienced leaders have learned that the best leaders don't talk the most, they do the most. Functioning leaders value planning and strategizing, but their pride is in executing their plan of action. They don't look for their name to be in lights; instead, their main objective is to perform at a high level, grow the people around them, and help the people around them in such a way that their lives change. If you grow and teach the people you serve daily, then, in return, you grow. There are a lot of returns in store for you.

In return, you become recognized. In return, you make money.

In return, titles come to you.

You won't find yourself chasing a title, but you will find yourself being chased by titles because you've functioned so well where you are.

I can recall when I was a sales consultant at the beginning of my career in retail. I wasn't the strongest salesperson, so I had to learn a way to become better and faster. My plan of action was to write down what my teammates did differently from me that caused them to win in sales. I had to learn and practice: I had to learn, then I had to practice how to articulate what I was doing differently from my peers. I needed to practice the things I did that made me successful. We called that the Secret Sauce. I also had to learn my peers' Secret Sauce. Once I figured out everyone's Secret Sauce, I shared it with the people around me. The more I shared it with the people around me, we all started to do better. We did better because we started to work together and coached each other up (we didn't wait for our boss to help us become better, we started coaching each other to get better based on our individual strengths and weaknesses). We didn't keep the Secret Sauce an actual secret – we shared! We developed a culture to serve each other and provide our customers with a fantastic experience.

No salesperson on the team worried that their customer dealt with incompetent employees, because the team was functioning at a high-level and holding each other to that high- level of performance expectation at all times. These are the types of positive behaviors that caused our store to reach record-breaking numbers. We became a store known for excellent customer service and high volume. Which of your peers are you willing to learn from? Who are you sharing best practices with? Are you humble enough to ask someone for help who is outperforming you? Peer to peer reviews are great ways to be developed without bringing your supervisors into the conversation. I had an accountability team when I was a district manager with almost 5 other district managers from all over the country. We had bi-weekly calls with each other to assist each other where we didn't have support from others.

We didn't allow anyone in the group to complain at all. We pushed each other to apply the behaviors that worked, and we coached each other up throughout the weeks. We developed a mini-culture of service and support by sharing the secret sauce. We couldn't have done this looking for someone at the top to make us better. We took our development into our own hands. You must start leading yourself before you can positively influence someone else.

As I shared the Secret Sauce, more people came to me for advice. The more I learned to serve (help others where I could), the more I realized I had to change my approach because my coaching and success led to my title starting to change. People began viewing me as a high-functioning leader. My peers saw me as the leader who cared, so I was sought out from the company and other businesses.

As I started to be sought out by more of my peers and noticed by some of our leaders, I started to become arrogant. In this arrogance, I bragged about my abilities to do great things and not bragging about the people I served who did the real work. I would get on phone calls just to hear people highlight what I was doing right. My attention and desires changed from developing people and sharing best practices to feeling entitled and showcasing my abilities. I started to become a person who desired a

"Title" more than I wanted to "Function" in my role. In this place, I started to put myself above everyone on my team.

What I've learned over time is we are fearless in pursuing success or our passions. Once we get what we're after or feel like we're near it, we drop the fearlessness and pick up fear of losing what we've worked to get. Fear of losing causes us to do things we wouldn't usually do. Out of fear of losing position, credit, notoriety, and so on, I bragged on myself. I didn't want to lose the little bit of attention I was getting. Fear of losing what I gained caused me to push for a title because I thought having a title would secure what I had. I've learned that titles don't secure position. Fear shouldn't be your driving force. I've watched people lead with fear as a way to drive results – it bred terrible behaviors. I've watched parents prevent their children from being all they can be due to fear.

I've seen people never leave their town out of fear of what's out there in the world, and I've also witnessed people become wealthy out of fear of struggling ever again. Because they've operated in that fear for so long, the most important thing in life becomes money; and, they'll do anything not to lose it – even at the expense of losing their family and friends. Author Peter Senge, states in his book The Fifth Discipline, "The tragedy is that many people who get hooked on conflict manipulation come to believe that only through being in a state of continual anxiety and fear can they be successful." You don't need fear to be successful or to get desired outcomes. You need willing people and a system to teach, train, coach, and reward them.

Chasing the title became my pursuit every day. It started to negatively affect my marriage and the way I raised my children. When I would come home from work, I expected my wife to serve me as opposed to me serving my wife. There were times when I could've stopped working and committed my time to my family, but I was in pursuit of a "Title," so I made an excuse to my family that I was working. My children started to make comments like, "Daddy is always working," or "We can't make any noise because daddy is on the phone again." I remember having a special dinner with my family and getting a phone call while at dinner. I stepped away from the table to answer the phone; and, by the time I realized how long I was on the phone, my family was walking out of the restaurant (they'd finished dinner). You could take this story and say I wouldn't want to work at a place like that. Your statement might be right for you. However, the job didn't make me make those decisions. I and many others didn't know what to value the most, so we made/make decisions like I did at dinner. Most businesses will not teach you how to have a balanced life, that's your responsibility. Functioning is being the best while on the clock, being the best when you're off the clock, and recognizing you need to balance both equally. Are you functioning when your responsibilities as an employer/employee are neglected because all you have focused on is your family? Or vice versa?

To end this chapter and get you thinking, I want to share some truths with you.

- If you live for others' acceptance, you'll die by their rejection.

- Commit to doing your best in your career because it's helping you to develop your brand. However, your family shouldn't be neglected for the sake of your career (have a balanced approach...you must use wisdom and you must use your vacation time). Please understand it works the other way around, also.

- If you're not happy where you are at work, still give your best at work while looking for something you want to do. Or, you can fall back in love with what you're doing by remembering why you started it in the first place. (The latter is what I'd always recommend you do first.)

- Find what you love to do in life and pursue that.

- Michael Moore said in an interview, "Don't become enamored with just getting promoted and moving up fast in an organization. Focus on getting a breadth of experiences. Lateral moves can be more important than being promoted, so that one day when you are in a leadership position, you want to be able to draw from your past experiences."

Please refer to the workbook to answer the questions concerning this chapter.

Continue to walk in greatness!

CHAPTER 12

GOOD VS. GREAT

We ended the last chapter with a statement that one of my mentors said. In essence, he said, "Don't miss your opportunity to be great because you've settled to be good. If you want to be great, you must value the experiences and learnings in life over the promotion." It's difficult to believe or apply this concept if you're in a financial crunch. It's also difficult to believe or apply the concept when you desire to have a title more than you want to function in your role.

However, what this is about is building a brand. Rome wasn't built overnight, and no one becomes excellent overnight.

There's an equation/pattern/rhythm/plan to be successful, just as there's an equation/pattern/rhythm/plan for failure. Every conversation, plan of action, reaction, relationship, setback, win, and perspective speaks to your current brand and will be the brand you're known for in the future. Society now is all about visual images; however, your brand has nothing to do with your appearance, yet. Your brand has everything to do with your behaviors and mentality.

Throughout the book so far, I've asked you a series of questions, and many of them have everything to do with your behaviors or how you're viewed based on your behaviors.

Behaviors and mentality will be the bridge that will get you from good to great. Your brand will be based on two major things, and we'll discuss them in more detail.

Mentality: Your perspective, how/why you think the way you do, and when you rest your brain.

Behaviors: What you do, how you do it, and when you do it. Behaviors also include your speech.

The mentality to move from good to great: When you look at an apple seed, what do you see? Most would only see an apple seed. Others would see an apple. A different group of people would see an apple tree. It's perspective. The difference between a janitor and the CEO is perspective. My uncle Russell Smyre used to tell me when I was younger, "Where your mind goes often enough, your body will soon follow." What statements do you hold close as your fire starter or rekindling statement? The statement my uncle shared with me made me reevaluate what was influencing my thoughts.

When I was a teenager, I would spend time driving around neighborhoods that were in the nicer areas (I was seeking out apple trees the best way I knew how). I didn't want what they had; instead, I needed to see something different from what I saw every day. My mother took my sisters and me on a cruise when we graduated from high school. She made sure we traveled, and she exposed us to as much as she could that was different from what we saw daily. What my mother did was stimulate my mind. She knew if I saw something greater than what I saw daily, I would push harder in life. Early in my marriage, I remember living in a two bedroom/one bath duplex. After work, I'd drive my wife around different neighborhoods, and we would discuss what type of home we wanted and which front doors we liked. It stimulated me to work hard because I had something to shoot for in life. I realized I was greater than my current situation, and I needed to prepare myself for what I wanted. I prepped!

With the combination of mentorship and diligent work to prove myself, the opportunities presented themselves. Of course, I maximized most of the opportunities! When I looked at my life, I didn't see an apple seed, I saw (and still see) not just an apple tree, but an apple orchard with thousands of apples filled with millions of apple seeds ready to be replanted after I put in the work and harvest them. We will discuss the harvest (behaviors/ work) and what it requires to move from good to great. Before we do, think about how your behaviors are influenced by how you view yourself. After all, this resource is about helping you to lead yourself as you lead others.

"Where your mind goes often enough, your body will soon follow." I have a good friend named Scott Brady; and, every day on social media, he posts a positive quote with his hashtag "be a better you." He's providing perspective for those who have the wrong perspective or don't have any at all. He believes the body will follow the mind. Who's influencing your thoughts? Who's going to push you to greatness if everyone around you is "good?" You need people around you who are walking in greatness, and you need inherently good people.

Greatness doesn't have a monetary value. Every so often on Tuesday and Thursday, my family and I connect with Matt and Caroline Nipper and their church to serve the under-resourced in our community. The Nippers and their church are great, in my eyes, because they have amazing hearts and serve people in need regularly. Helping others isn't a one-time main event; it's the way they live. We hold each other to serving those in need. The Nippers challenge the way I think, which influences how I see myself and my behaviors. The Nippers and Scott Brady are great people in my eyes. They challenge me to be great, among so many others. It's always a good thing when you're not the smartest person in the room.

Behaviors to move from good to great: Keep in mind the statement my uncle shared with me, "Where your mind goes often enough, your body will soon follow." I recall being young and pretending that I was sick. I remember faking like I was sick, then I ended up being sick for real. I believed this false reality so much that my body reacted to it. I've heard about false pregnancy in women and sympathy pains in men, so I did a quick web search. What I found on WebMD is that false pregnancy, clinically termed Pseudocyesis, is the belief that you are expecting a baby when you are not carrying a child. People with pseudocyesis have many, if not all, symptoms of pregnancy with the expectation of an actual fetus. Men experience a form of Pseudocyesis when they gain weight with their spouse during pregnancy and when they feel sympathy pains. This is just like my Uncle's quote! Your mind will determine where you go and how far you will go. Your cognitive domain will define why you behave the way you do.

Behavior isn't only physical action; it also includes your conversation. I teach my team my leadership statement: "Worthwhile conversations will bring about worthwhile relationships. Worthwhile relationships will give you access. Access allows you influence." You cannot correct your actions/behaviors without correcting your thought process. If you can't visualize yourself in a better place in life doing something greater (in your eyes), you'll sabotage yourself when the opportunity presents itself. Here are ways you prevent yourself from moving from good to great:

- Complacency: You get comfortable where you are. When you get comfortable, you start to miss things you'd normally catch. You don't push as hard because you've "made it." You've built a system so now you can coast. Keep this truth in mind, "You can only coast going downhill, not when you're doing the climb."

- Entitlement: You start to believe you deserve what you have and because you deserve it, it cannot be taken from you. When you start to feel entitled, your work ethic starts to dissolve. You'll stop being a student of your craft nor will you put any time and energy into developing the next generation.

- Being a solo act: You did this on your own. You got to where you are on your own, and no one did anything to assist you. No one thought, worked, invested, encouraged, or supported you along the way. You're completely selfish at this point, and everyone is less than you. I had a friend some years ago who entered into relationship after relationship. They were all sour! They were very toxic relationships, and they always ended before they escalated to something that would involve the authorities. He said to me, "Man, there aren't any good ladies out here anymore. Every relationship I've been in is bad." He went on and on and on about how the ladies were bad, and he was good.

I laughed in disbelief. I asked one simple question, "Friend, in all of your relationships, what's the common denominator?" I suggested that he look at the common denominator and correct it, then his life would be better including his love life. He treated every relationship like it was just him, and the other person was tagging along for the ride. Many of us do this in leadership, in our relationships, at work, in our business, with our peers. What a selfish way of thinking! We did not get where we are alone, whether it's good or bad. We don't do it on our own.

Individuals who can envision themselves doing great work don't always wait for the opportunity; some create the opportunities for themselves. Can you see yourself where you want to be? I'd like to give you a few words, if coupled with your plan, will drive you from good to great.

1. Competency: If you love what you do, at least love it enough to educate yourself on it. It's not enough to just like doing it. Good people do what they like, great people do what they love; and, to function at the highest level in it, they educate themselves. I'm a huge supporter of education. However, learning your craft doesn't necessarily mean going to school. You can get a mentor, take classes for a certificate, attend seminars, complete virtual courses, read books, volunteer your time to see it done the right way, just to name a few.

2. <u>Consistency:</u> To move from good to great you must execute what you're doing more consistently than your peers and at a higher level than your peers. Scared money doesn't make money. Keep fighting for your dream, and don't be afraid to lose. If you want to be a great basketball player, you can't be afraid to miss a shot. If you want to succeed in life, you can't be afraid to fail. When you find the winning formula, stick to it!

3. <u>Practice:</u> The greats in any area of life aren't ignorant when it comes to what they do.

They're performing at a high level more consistently than their peers because they're practicing at a high level more consistently than their peers. Jerry Rice is known as one of the greatest wide receivers ever in NFL history.

Amongst his peers and coaches, he's known as one of the best-trained players ever. He was an expert in training and practicing to develop himself to be the best. Are you known for your ability to practice like Jerry was? It is the same for greats such as Michael Jordan, Lebron James, Michael Jackson, Zig Ziglar, John Maxwell, Tom Brady, and so on. All of the greats continue to practice running the plays, reciting their sales pitch, evaluating themselves, greeting people at the door, overcoming objections, rehearsing their sermons, racing their cars around the track, etc. If the greats were already great and still practiced, so should you!

I believe we're like the apple seed, we all have an apple orchard inside us just waiting to be harvested. The reality is, everyone will not nurture the seed that lives inside of them to get the greatest potential out of it. However, you can! But it's a choice...your choice! The difference between someone who's considered great and someone who isn't is their ability to choose to be great and commit to doing what's necessary to achieve that goal. Do you choose to be great? Do you have the mentality of a great? Show the world with your actions and behaviors, instead of lip service or appearance!

Please refer to the workbook to answer the questions concerning this chapter.

CHAPTER 13

THE BUMP

When my wife and I were newlyweds, we boarded a ship cruising to Cabo San Lucas for our honeymoon. We were still high on life because less than 48 hours before, we said "I do" to each other. I recall being on the ship finishing dinner with my wife and deciding that we would relax a little by dancing. Page and I hit the dance floor, and it was going great. We were in sync, two-stepping all over that dance floor. I noticed that a few couples stopped to watch us dance. There was another couple on the ship dancing alongside us. It was great until they bumped into us in the middle of the dance floor! My response was laughter, but I noticed something: Every time we were bumped, we were knocked off rhythm. I had to stop dancing, assess the situation, and then resume dancing again. Once I pulled it together, we danced the night away.

This chapter is dedicated to the individuals who have already started to move toward what they want in life, but in the process got bumped by something or someone. The bump, in context to this chapter, is a setback, missed opportunity, lapse in your integrity, bad decision, marital conflict, financial struggle, or lack of knowledge. I can relate the bump to different situations in my life during different time frames. The idea of this chapter is to help you develop a mindset that will cause you to push forward when the pressures of this life start to pull you back – bump you and knock you out of your rhythm.

Naturally, I'm an optimist. I always see the glass full, I'm always looking for the good in individuals, and I believe everyone deserves an opportunity to be coached or developed before they're cut off. The way you handle bumps, roadblocks, and obstacles in your life will be based on your perspective. Perspective is defined as a particular attitude toward, or way of regarding, something; a point of view.

Perspective is essential vision and recovery.

The first area of perspective is Vision. Remember, Chapter 1 covered having a dream and waking up to make that dream reality. You'd never pursue your dream if you didn't think you could do it. You must believe you can do this! No matter what anyone says to you about reaching your dreams, your perspective must be, "I can and will do this. If I don't know how to win, I'll learn how to win, but I will and can do this!" Many people, like myself, have affirmation statements that we recite every morning and when we get discouraged. We recite these statements to get our heads back in the game when we're falling apart internally. Having daily affirmations will help you gain perspective of your goals. You can't let go of your perspective if it's positive and pushing you toward your dream. Outlook is the intangible item to start you moving toward your dream.

The second area of perspective is Recovery. Recovery is the process of regaining control of something that was lost or stolen. There's not a person on this planet who hasn't lost something on this journey called life. The people we believe to be successful didn't let a bump stop them from moving forward. I know great athletes who've been injured, and they couldn't play their sport anymore (which means they didn't get money or needed a new career). I know great business owners who didn't have money to handle their payroll (financial loss). I know great people who've had a lapse in their integrity (lost trust). I know great people who've just made a bad business move (lost everything). I know great people who've lost loved ones (lost faith). Of the group of people I've listed, the ones who didn't lose their perspective were able to bounce back from any bump. They recovered!

Here are some of my go-to examples of recovery:

- I remember reading Dave Ramsey's book about financial wisdom. I pay attention to his writings because he became a millionaire from nothing, lost it all, and regained it back by maintaining his perspective and following some essential principles.

- Jamisha Rinnix is a fantastic woman that can fight. She beat stage 4 ovarian cancer in 2014. She's never lost perspective of her faith and relationship with God. She recovered from that bump and is now helping others beat cancer. A true inspiration!

- My former leader and CEO was a person I've paid close attention to for more than 10 years of my adult life. He's the Founder and Executive Chairman of arguably the largest retailer for Verizon. He ran into some difficult times early on as a CEO. That bump didn't stop him; he surrounded himself with a coach and people to help him grow his business. He said in an interview, "Hiring a CEO coach was probably the number one thing that I did to help turn my company around. Second was joining the Young Presidents' Organization and continuing my education as both a president of a company and just as an overall father, parent, husband, just getting to be a better person in general." I'm a fan!

Each of the individuals I've mentioned above has lost something or didn't have all they needed to run the race of life like many of us believe. The one thing they maintained in life was their perspective, no matter what was lost. We must keep in mind they lost a lot in life, and each of them would tell you they have. They'd also tell you that when times were difficult, they had a support team around them to keep pushing them.

They maintained their perspective after being down for a while. They recovered!

When I get bumped at work or in life, I step back and assess the situation or project. I take a look at everything contributing to what I'm doing, and I evaluate it all. After I'm able to identify the successes and areas of opportunities (failures), I build a plan of action. The plan of action may be to stop what I'm doing, tweak the plan, or bring in some help. No matter what it is, I'll have a better understanding once I evaluate what I've done. It's critical that you understand there's a time lapse I haven't spoken about in assessing the situation. Sometimes the evaluation will take a week to complete, yet, sometimes I evaluate and determine a corrective strategy right then and there on the spot. It depends on the situation and the due date.

You are great and are doing great things in life. You're changing your life and the life of others daily. Bounce back and lead on! Please refer to the workbook to answer the questions concerning this chapter.

CHAPTER 14

BIBLICAL PERSPECTIVE

Not my will but yours: I don't know about you, but there are situations in life where I excel above average, and people around me are in awe of my performance. During those times I think to myself, "I got this!" Everyone around me, think I got it, just as I said to myself; but, the reality was that I didn't have anything in my control. I had to realize that the great things people saw in me weren't because I was great; instead, they were because of the great work that Jesus completed in me, just as He did in you. He gave me these talents and skills to provide a platform to showcase His grace, love, kindness, and forgiveness. If it were about me (my will), I'd use the platform to do other things like control people, influence others to do what's best for me, abuse the access I have to people's hearts and money, and neglect my wife and children in pursuit of my own agenda. I don't do those things because I'm committed to God only!

In the book of Matthew 26:36-56 (NIV) of the Holy Bible, Jesus was in the garden praying because he knew what he had to do. While praying, he says, "My Father if it is possible, may this cup be taken from me. Not as I will, but as you will." It didn't show that Jesus was a coward, it showed his humanity. It showed he wanted to explore other options if there were any, but there weren't. So in the same breath, he says, "it's not my will but yours." Jesus submitted to the will of God over his own will. In other words, he took God's will and made it his own. Because of his commitment to the will of the Father over his own, his belief dictated his behaviors.

Whether or not you believe in Jesus as God, there's a truth here I want to share with you. You behave according to what you believe. Jesus believed he had to die for the sins of the world, so his actions accompanied his belief. What do you believe at your core? What's your purpose for waking up in the mornings? It should be more than to make a dollar because that's vain. What are you making money for? Do your actions line up with what you believe?

I used to ask my reps who underperformed, why do you come to work every day? Many of them would say, "To provide for my family." I thought that was admirable, and I would let them know that. But, my next questions were, "Why don't your actions reflect what you believe?" One rep started crying and said, "No one has ever told me my actions are a reflection of what I believe!" That rep's actions changed immediately afterward. The rep started studying sales behaviors, and the rep started to practice more. Now that rep is managing a store and having the same conversation with others. Your behaviors are driven by what you believe.

Elijah and Elisha: According to the Bible (1 Kings 19:19-21), Elisha was working on his family farm. He knew there was more to life than what he was experiencing. (I know so many of you can relate to this story already!) One day the great Prophet Elijah walked by. In his heart, Elisha knew he was supposed to be mentored by Elijah. Elisha believed it so much that he dropped his plow and followed Elijah to be trained. Elisha didn't want a title; he wanted to function. He wanted to help others by serving them. He realized that Elijah was functioning at a high level, he desired to do the same, so he dropped everything to be discipled by the great Prophet.

Please don't confuse mentorship with discipleship. We all need to be mentored in business. We also need to be discipled, which is the development of your spiritual life. Both are important, one will carry you through this life, and the other will make you a better person in this life and prepare you for life after death. My parallel story: I knew I was supposed to be a leader of leaders; so, when my peers were partying, I was studying; when my friends focused on dating, I was building business relationships; and, when I saw a person who was doing what I wanted, I asked them to mentor me. Most of my mentors in business have a relationship with God. I don't look to them for spiritual guidance; but, in many cases, they've provided me with great counsel spiritually. I have a Pastor who helps me spiritually and close friends in the faith that hold me accountable spiritually. I need both to continue to grow in both areas of my life.

All things work together for the good: If you ate a couple of raw eggs with a side cup of flour and a couple sticks of butter, it would be disgusting! However, if you take those same ingredients with a few other ingredients, mix them, and apply some heat you'll get a nice pound cake. Our life is the same! Romans 8:28 speaks to this principle in that Paul said, "all things work together for the good." We don't know the exact ingredients God will use in our lives – some ingredients could be a new job, loss of a job, hardship, success, financial freedom, terminal illness, car accidents, rough childhood, and so on. We don't know, but I do believe God will take all the ingredients in our lives and make them work out for our good. The heat from an oven alone is hot and potentially dangerous.

However, when you put the correct ingredients under the correct temperature, you can get a cake, muffins, pies, and more.

It's important for you to understand that if you go through a hard time or have a bad year, it will eventually work out. All you must do is continue to learn, remain humble, take action, and trust that God will make sure it works out for your good. You and I cannot control everything that happens to us in life; but, the one thing we can control is our perspective.

We have as much control as a flea flying in the middle of a hurricane. No matter what happens in life, we must maintain our perspective and believe it will all work out. The flea flying in the hurricane can say, "I have no control over my life, and now this crazy wind has damaged all I have." Or it could say, "I needed to get across town, and with the assistance of this crazy wind I'm going to get there without having to exhaust myself." All things will work together for your good.

Do you have the perspective to back what you believe?

Take time to complete the section in the workbook for this chapter.

PART IV
QUALITY CONTROL

Reminder: This resource is for the individual who has dreams and has yet to wake up and create their desired reality. This resource is also for the individual who's started moving toward their end goal but somehow stopped making forward progress.

CHAPTER 15

QC: SELF-EVALUATION

What good is it to attend a sporting event if we cannot keep score? The crossovers in basketball, the tackles in football, the triple jumps in ice skating, or the famous figure four in wrestling (I'm dating myself with that one) are great; but, if we don't have a winner at the end of those famous moves, it's not as exciting to watch. Quality Control (QC) is about keeping score. Many people don't think about keeping score when it comes to life. But, we see it every day in the business world. We must beat our year-over-year numbers, and we must show gradual growth month-over-month. The Bible speaks of people examining themselves (checking our character to make sure we're right morally, ethically, and spiritually). Someone once asked me, "How do you know what the standard is or when you're right or not?" You have a coach or mentor who will assist you in seeing what right looks like. There will be a few of you who will not have a blueprint – you will be the blueprint for those to come after you. Steve Jobs, Lecrae, the Wright Brothers,

Martin Luther King, Jr., James Cameron, and many more have created new paths that no other person has created. They've had mentors and coaches during their journey and have become the coaches/mentors of others.

When you look at your life, how do you view yourself and your quality? Eric Boles said, "You can view life from the perspective of a fan or the perspective of a coach." There's so much truth to what Boles said. Once I heard his statement, I looked at life differently, especially when it comes to how I evaluate the way I plan, execute, and follow up. Let's dig into this statement a little more. To provide you some context, let's look at when you're watching a sporting event, and your favorite team wins. Most fans will take the win, brag on their team, and highlight their favorite plays. The fan is more excited about the win. The fan doesn't have insight into how the plays were constructed or if the players are executing at their best. It's entertainment for the fan. However, the coach has a different perspective: The coach will take the win, brag about how the team pulled it together to gain the win, and will highlight the missed opportunities for the team to play better in the next game. This game isn't entertainment to the coach – it's an opportunity to witness how well they've coached and how well the team executed. The coach knows each play and each player intimately so they can question each player's level of commitment.

I've learned to evaluate myself weekly. My end goal is to re-evaluate myself, daily, as my mentor is challenging me to do. How often are you evaluating yourself? Sports teams review themselves after practice and after games. Business professionals review themselves every day to get the best results by the end of the month. Schedule time for yourself to be honest with yourself. Additionally, schedule regular meetings with your coach (who will be proud of your progress, but not impressed) to be challenged, coached, and realigned. Your end goal will not mean anything if you don't evaluate your progress and beat yourself month-over-month and year-over-year.

The evaluation process can easily become an award ceremony based on how you make yourself feel that month, week, or day. It's not a proper evaluation unless you measure how you feel after every task. If your end goal is to feel better about yourself, be warned: we're not really touching on feelings in this book. So, to effectively grade yourself, you must establish some objective standards – targets that you cannot lie to yourself about accomplishing or give excuses if you miss the mark.

I measure behaviors (my actions) and outcomes (the result of my actions). As you start to evaluate yourself consistently, you'll become more critical of your behaviors, and you'll recognize what outcomes happen when you fully commit versus when you're not fully committed. By measuring behaviors and outcomes, you keep it clean by speaking to what you did or didn't do and what happened or didn't happen based on YOU. For example, when I wanted to sell a product, I measured myself on casting vision, delivering training content, a two-week deadline, product availability, clearing the path, following up on training, performance management, celebrating our wins, correcting loss, and so on. By following this system I've produced at a level high enough to be promoted within the company, I work for, develop my own business, mentor others and their success based on this format, and build a nice life for my family...all of this by the grace of God. I will not and cannot take responsibility for my success on my own. I can only take credit for my level of commitment and my ability to listen to others who've already walked where I want to go.

Evaluation will help you to become a better person in two ways: coachability and humility. First, you become or remain coachable. As long as you allow someone to coach you, you remain coachable and valuable to others. The moment you can't be coached, you lose your value in many ways and become a tyrant. All great people and leaders have a great skill called listening. Everyone around you shouldn't agree with everything you say or do. I'm a listener – a student– so I'm critical (think analyzer, not criticizer) of my leaders. I don't challenge them, but I don't agree with everything they do either. I follow them and will continue to because I'm not supposed to agree with everything they do. That doesn't take away from the fact that they are great leaders. I have my own perspective on many situations that vary from their perspective. My leadership team listens to my perspective because they value it. However, that doesn't mean they will do whatever I suggest. Do you allow the people who follow you a chance to speak or make suggestions? If not, why? Most people just want to be heard; and, often, a suggestion box will fulfill that need. If you'd like to take it a step further, implement a great idea, and you'll win the hearts of the people following you. When my leadership team suggests I do something, I do it because they have my best interest at heart and want to develop me to be where they are someday. I'm viewed as coachable, are you?

Second, you become or remain humble. Unless you have the mindset to want to be better at what you do, you will not be open to being corrected on a regular basis. Let me pause here and say that coaching and abuse are two different things. I've been in situations where bosses verbally abuse their people by using profanity toward them, telling them they suck, and threatening to take their job away to get better results. I've also had some of the greatest leaders who've told me I've dropped the ball and showed me how to correct that.

They encouraged me and asked me questions to make me really think about the business. I've had great leaders who've said I wasn't ready to step up and some who've said I wasn't confident when I should be. When you know you don't have all the answers, and you don't have it all together, you're humble. Humble isn't less than, rather it is an attitude of gratitude for where you are and what you have. When you're humble, you show your appreciation by committing yourself completely to the cause. When you're humble, you don't accept failure. However, you're more likely to extend grace to others by making sure you do your part of developing them.

RE-VISIT THE ORIGINAL PLAN

As a part of evaluating yourself and your progress, you will need to bump your progress against the vision. The reality is that your plan will evolve based on your progress. Your plan will evolve as you learn more about the ins and outs of what you want to do. It will also change based on your growth and development. Don't lose sight of your "what" and "why." The core of your end goal is going to be wrapped up in "why" you're doing "what" you're doing. Over time, you may change what you're doing to better support your "why." Don't allow that to be a reason to stop what you're doing if it's working.

I'll provide you with a real situation. I had to revisit why I started writing this book. Originally, I was on this leadership kick and wanted to help develop leaders in business to be more human and organized. However, when I started to do some research and looked at myself, I realized I wanted to help individuals become a leader in and of themselves, so they could become a leader of others. There are many books on how to be successful and how to become wealthy. I believe we must learn to manage the way we think, plan, act, and view ourselves if we want to be successful and have a balanced life. If we can get our hands wrapped around that idea, we'd be in a better place to accomplish our goals and help others do the same.

The issues derive from not knowing who you are. When parents know who they are, they will be intentional about making sure their children learn who they are before they leave the house. Children who know who they are will less likely to try to fit in. They believe they can set the new trends, they're more respectful, and they work harder because they have a better understanding of the brand they carry...their last name. Additionally, children who know who they are don't bully and will stand up for kids who are being bullied. It starts with the parents.

It took me months to come to this conclusion after I'd already started building out my plan of execution. And, of course, I had to make some tweaks. My "why" has never changed; my "what" has grown larger; and, my "how" has evolved to simply becoming a great communicator. How I communicate will be varied, but I aim to clearly communicate my "why." When I say I'm a communicator, people see that as a singular thing; however, it could be communicating through this book, a workbook, a blog, a television sitcom, a keynote address, mentoring, teaching, and many other ways. In my past, I would've put each way I communicate down on paper to show someone – it would've been one way only. After years of thought and learning, I'm a multi-faceted communicator. The way I communicate will vary at times, but it's communication nevertheless. When I revisited the progress of this book against the plan, I realized I'd grown, and my perspective was different. I was better at consolidating my vision into one statement.

If you need to make changes to your plan as you're revisiting the original plan, that's okay. Don't beat yourself up! I remember being a District Manager about to open a new store. We had the plans to build out this new store a certain way. Weeks into the buildout, we realized our original plans wouldn't work. We continued with the "what" (open the new store), we continued with the why (extend the footprint and make more money), but we changed the "how" (instead of 4 working stations we did 6). The plan changed slightly, but we finished and completed the what.

Earlier in my career, I had the privilege of having a few conversations with Ralph Ketner. Ralph Ketner was a great businessman and philanthropist. He was known for being the founder of Food Lion in 1957.

Mr. Ketner asked me one day, "Do you have a house?" "No sir, I don't," I said.

"Do you want one?" he asked.

"Mr. Ketner, I plan on buying one," I replied.

He said, "If you want to buy something new, create a new revenue stream to pay for it."

At that point, my "how" changed for everything. I was

listening to a man who started this huge grocery store chain from nothing. Because he did it, I knew I could do it! Now, that's the standard for me. If I want something new, I need to create another revenue stream to pay for it. He provided me with a nugget that challenged me and changed me. I have so many great people who have challenged me and changed me.

Who's influencing your life and what do you have to show for that? Some of the people who influenced me to change my plan are successful monetarily, and there are some rich in peace, enjoying faithful marriages, declaring contentment and joy, feeling fulfillment in serving the needy, and so much more! I have a diverse group that influences me so I can be more well- rounded. Don't be easily influenced by anyone. Be picky about who you let change your mind. Even if it's you.

RE-VISIT THE STEPS

One of my favorite sections in this book is the Steps. We must revisit the steps often. This behavior does two things great and can do one thing harmful. The two great things it will do are to help you celebrate and encourage yourself.

Revisiting the steps will help you celebrate your wins. You can't look back at accomplishing anything if there's nothing to look back on. You must continue moving.

I was cycling in a triathlon, and it was my first time. I

was cycling up this extremely difficult hill. So I looked at the ground in front of me and never looked up because it was too much to take in at once. I peddled to move past the ground in front of me, foot-by-foot until I got to the top of the hill. Once I got to the top of the hill, as I was going down, I screamed as I mentally looked back. I celebrated conquering that hill!

The second great thing revisiting the steps will do is encourage you. After conquering that hill, I was encouraged to continue the race. That was the first of two major hills in that triathlon. The second hill was a fight, but I went up the second hill with a better mindset than I did going up the first. I'd beaten the first hill, so I knew I could beat the second hill.

Those two points bring me to a phrase I want to share with you. We've covered this earlier in the book, but it warrants another visit. It is the attitude of gratitude! I'm alive today to make a better decision than I made yesterday, so I have an attitude of gratitude. I could focus on who didn't help me or what caused me to be in a better place. Most people will spend their entire life talking about what they don't have and how they were wronged. I'm not here to debate those struggles. I'm talking about taking control over the controllables in your life which are your perspective and being grateful for where you are now. Be grateful for the ones who have helped you by encouraging you through words or deed. When you're able to say, "I own today moving forward," you take your life out of the hands of others, and you become responsible for your actions. As I was cycling up those hills, every single rider who passed me said encouraging words like, "Don't stop, keep pushing, one stroke at a time, and I'll see you at the finish line." There were people on the side of the street and every corner saying, "You got this, you're almost there," and more. These people represent all the good in your life. You might not be able to change your environment right now, but you can change who you allow to speak life, encouraging words, and wisdom into your life. Learn your patterns as you revisit the steps. There's always something to be learned from the steps of life.

There's one harmful part of revisiting the steps. That harmful part is when you don't learn from what you see when you revisit the steps. When you look back over your life, what are you looking for? Are you looking to highlight all the negative things that have happened to you? Are you looking to ignore your past? Are you looking for missed opportunities?

What patterns are you looking for in your behavior? (Some of us need professional assistance with overcoming and learning ways to handle what's happened to us in our past. I'm not minimizing those situations. If you find that this applies to you, please seek professional assistance.)

I revisit the steps in my life to celebrate wins, encourage myself, and learn my behavioral patterns. Only when I looked back on my life did I realize that for many years, during September and October, I would fall into a slump and not push as hard as I normally would. It wasn't until years later that I realized I struggled with adapting to work, managing school, and handling other obligations all at the same time. It all happened annually during these months. I felt overwhelmed and would get so exhausted that my level of commitment was subpar. I had to learn delegation and time management. If I had never revisited the steps, I would have never picked up on that pattern to correct it later. As we're learning about everything else, don't forget to learn yourself in the process. At the same time, don't spend too much time revisiting the steps. You can't drive forward while keeping your eyes fixed on the rearview mirror. Quickly looking back to analyze the steps and to tweak your plan will be your start to Quality Control. Let's finish strong by completing the workbook to answer the questions concerning this chapter.

FINAL THOUGHTS

Years ago, I was asked to move from one state to another state for work. It was the first time I moved for work. I lived near family all my life, so this was a first for my wife, children, and me. Before Page and I made the decision to move, I had a conversation with a mentor at the time. He said, "Nate, some great people can do what you can do. There are some who might even do it better than you would. The truth here is their house isn't right. Because your house is right, you're better prepared to maximize this opportunity." I will never forget that statement! What I took from that statement was: if I didn't cast a vision for my family or prepare them for opportunities for success, we'd always miss the chance for growth.

Today I interpret the same statement differently. Today the statement means: I must first be able to have a vision for myself, I must clear the path for myself, and I must inspect what I expect from myself. If I can learn to discipline myself to think ahead, strategize, execute a plan, and evaluate my progress objectively, there won't be an issue with me leading any group of people. The real struggle is that we've never been taught how to become disciplined individuals. We read books and take classes on ways to gain wealth, start a business, and lead groups of people without first understanding how to control our thoughts, be content with who we are, or learn to use the resources available to us. My prayer and hope is that after reading this book, you've become more disciplined in how you evaluate yourself, strategize a plan, execute, and view yourself.

I'll end with the sentiment I opened the book with, "This book is for individuals who have dreams and have yet to wake up and create the reality they desire. This book is also for the individual who's started moving toward the end goal but somehow stopped making forward progress." Every chapter in this book is based on true stories and events. Every principle or behavior written in this book has been put to use, and my life has changed for the better because of the application of these behaviors. I've witnessed others grow tremendously as I shared the same ideas in mentorship sessions. If you've taken anything away from this book, I pray it's that you've gained some forward momentum. With that momentum, a few of the next moves you make will become easier. However, don't stop evaluating yourself, so you keep that momentum. As a part of the evaluation process I conduct on myself, I stop everything and listen to your feedback. Help me in this evaluation process by providing feedback about your experience with reading this book. Let me know if it was beneficial to you and how. Let me know if it wasn't beneficial at all. Your feedback is a part of how I evaluate myself and the material I use to coach others.

I want to leave you with my leadership statement: "Worthwhile conversations will bring about worthwhile relationships. Worthwhile relationships will give you access. Access allows you influence." - Nathaniel Woods, Jr.

Lead on, starting with you!

ACKNOWLEDGMENTS

I'd like to thank everyone who's assisted me with this project. Dr. PageCarol Woods, you've been the best support, confidant, wife, and mother to our children. Thank you for transcribing more than 80% of this project and being a sounding board for me. Dr. Amy Bratten, thank you for being a great friend and editor for this project. We have many more projects to go. Sarah MacDonald, thank you for managing this project and so many more. We're incredibly blessed to have you in our lives. To my parents (Linda & Virgil Knight and Nathaniel Woods Sr.), thanks for raising me and teaching me many of the values I share in this book. To my sisters and brothers (Tosha, Iesha, Genia, Westley, Elijah, Iman, Marcel, and Gordon), you've always encouraged me, provided so many ideas, and more than anything you help keep me grounded. I love and appreciate you guys so much. Brad Penley, I can't express how much I appreciate your wisdom, confidence, support, and accountability. Kadreana Mack, Solon Flowers, Michael Moore and Mauro Davila thank you for proofing the manuscript and providing candid feedback. There are many more individuals that believe in me and the work that I'm doing. For your belief and support, thank you, thank you, thank you. Finally, thank you to every person that has purchased this book.

REFERENCE

Exclusive Q&a: Victra Chief Experience Officer - Retail ... (n.d.). Retrieved from https://www.retailtouchpoints. com/topics/shopper- experience/exclusive-q-a-victra

False Pregnancy (pseudocyesis) - Webmd. (n.d.). Retrieved from https://www.webmd.com/baby/ false-pregnancy- pseudocyesis

Sanduski, S. (2015, May 5), Re: Rich Balot on... the 5 things every ceo should focus on [web log message]. Retrieved from http://ceocoachinginternational.com

Senge, P. (2006). The fifth discipline: The art and practice of the learning organization (Rev. and updated. ed., A currency book). New York: Doubleday/Currency.

Sonic boom. 2018. In Merriam-Webster.com. Retrieved June 3, 2018, from https://www.merriam-webster.com/dictionary/sonicboom

DOTS:
Developing Others
Through Service

Starting with ME!

WORKBOOK

INTRODUCTION

This book is for individuals who have dreams and have yet to wake up and create the reality they desire. This book is also for the individual who's started moving toward the end goal but somehow stopped making forward progress.

Keep this in mind as you read through each section of the book.

Do you have an end goal in mind for your life? If so, what is it?

_____

_____

If not, what is the vision for yourself?

_____

_____

I missed many opportunities in my past because of this four-letter word. What is the four-letter word?

"The wealthiest place in the world," Dr. Monroe declared, "is not the gold mines of South America or the oil fields of Iraq or Iran. They are not the diamond mines of South Africa or the banks of the world. The wealthiest place on the planet is just down the road. It is the cemetery. There lie buried companies that were never started, inventions that were never made, bestselling books that were never written, and masterpieces that were never painted. In the cemetery is buried the greatest treasure of untapped potential. Don't go to the grave with your treasure still in you!" - Dr. Myles Monroe

What are you dreaming about?

_____

_____

What are you afraid of?

_____

_____

How is your fear of _____

_____, preventing your dream from becoming reality?

Maybe your goal isn't to be wealthy beyond your wildest dreams or to start a business. Maybe your dream is to be a better spouse. Maybe your dream is to volunteer once a week as a way of giving back. No matter what your dream is, you must wake up to bring it to fruition.

CHAPTER 1

EVENTUALLY, YOU MUST WAKE UP!

Having a dream about where you want to be is a great thing and will build hope as long as you know you can make it happen. But, when you don't see movement in real life getting you closer to your dream, different emotions breed. You become anxious and impatient; and, you feel like you're in a nightmare.

Dreaming is simply a way to visualize what you want internally. However, to move forward and bring the dream to reality, you must wake up. The longer you stay in the dream state without forward progress, the faster your dream will turn into a nightmare.

Below are a few questions to trigger you to wake up:

1.   What are you visualizing in your dream?

_____

_____

2.   Are you spending more time dreaming than you are working toward the dream? If so, how is excessive dreaming helping you?

_____

_____

3.   How much time do you set aside to fulfilling your dream daily?

_____

_____

4.   What are you doing with the time you've scheduled daily?

_____

_____

5.   Do you spend more time on social media looking at other people's lives than you do making your life worth watching?

_____

_____

6.   Are you investing in yourself? If so, what things are you doing to invest in yourself?

_____

_____

Wake up! Wake up! Wake up!

CHAPTER 2

WRITE OUT THE PLAN

You must always begin with the end in mind.

Let me be clear before we go any further: you can work for someone your entire life and complete your own goals. Not everyone is cut out to be self-employed or a business owner; but, you don't have to quit your day job to fulfill your heart's desires.

For some of you reading this book, your place of employment will be the source of income to help you move to greatness – just make sure you have a winning budgeting plan.

1. Why are you getting out of bed every day?

_____

_____

2. Are you content or complacent where you are in life right now? If content, why? If complacent, why?

_____

_____

3. Why are you punching the clock at work every day?

_____

_____

4. Why don't you have a vision for yourself? Or, do you? What is it?

_____

_____

5. Why are you assisting someone else accomplish their personal goals and without focusing on yours?

_____

_____

Activity: Write out all the steps you'd take to make a peanut butter and jelly sandwich. - I'd like to ask you a few questions so you'd think about your PB&J process (no need to answer these questions – think about the process you're writing out).

o Where did you get the bread from?

_____

o Where did you open the jelly?

_____

o How did you get from the place of the silverware to
   the place where you make your sandwich?

_____

o Did you clean up?

_____

I have a series of questions to ask you to help you establish
your "how."

1. How do you plan to achieve your goal or reach your
    mark – what are the milestones (remember PB&J)?

_____

_____

2. What support do you need to achieve each milestone?

_____

_____

3. How will you get the support for each milestone?

_____

_____

4. How will achieving each milestone get you closer to your end goal?

_____

_____

Earlier in the chapter, I mentioned the "what" is the vehicle by which you will get to your end goal. I always start with the "why" and "how" of the vehicle. Once I have a solid response to the "why" and "how", the true "what" is revealed.

We all have ideas of things we want to accomplish in life. We don't get traction on these items without considering why we're doing it, how we're going to do it, or if it makes sense to do it at all. Below are a series of questions that I hope will challenge you to think about your approach to life:

1. What do you want to do in life?

_____

_____

2. Do you have a guide to follow (mentor)?

_____

_____

3. Who are they? Are they willing to help you?

_____

_____

4. How much time do you need to achieve your end goal?

_____

_____

5. Who is/are your accountability partner(s) along this journey?

_____

_____

CHAPTER 3

GET CONNECTED

This chapter is heavy so I've provided space for you to gather your thoughts.

_____

_____

_____

_____

_____

_____

_____

_____

Who are you connected to?

_____

_____

Are you being mentored (being a student, willing to learn
from someone else)?

_____

_____

Are you being a mentor to someone else? Why?

_____

_____

What is the mentee getting out of the relationship and
what are you getting out of the relationship?

_____

_____

CHAPTER 4

BIBLICAL PERSPECTIVE

Area 1:

James 1: 22 says, "But be doers of the word, and not hearers only, deceiving yourselves."

What scriptures or readings do you pull from that challenges you to stay honest with yourself?

_____

_____

How would you describe a person that is a hearer only and not a doer? Are you describing yourself in any area of your life?

_____

_____

Area 2:

One of the founders of the United States, Alexander Hamilton once said, "If you don't stand for something you'll fall for nothing." Having vision or a goal in mind will help direct your behaviors. Steph Curry who is arguably one of the greatest shooters in the NBA has a vision to be one of the greatest in the NBA. His vision determines the level of work he puts in during practice. During practice one of his shooting drills is to take 100 shots from the 3-point line. That's one drill. He practices pivots and pick-and-roll foot work because he realizes these are actionable items he do every night at a high frequency. The Vision you have should dictate your responses. You need to take the next year to focus on you and becoming a better you before going back into another relationship. That's the vision. If you realize you're becoming dependent on drinking or smoking or whatever your vice is and you're ready to stop letting that addiction control you.

What is your vision? To have a better quality of life?

_____

_____

How would you practice that daily?

_____

The vision will determine your actions.

135

Area 3:

Who do you know that's completed a task like what you desire to do?

_____

_____

Have you asked them for guidance?

_____

_____

I'll provide you with part of my leadership statement that will help you immensely: *"Worthwhile conversations will bring about worthwhile relationships..."* Asking for guidance isn't about the guidance as much as it is about a genuine relationship with the individual. The relationship will provide you more than a ten-minute conversation every other week with tips.

CHAPTER 5

SONIC BOOM

What conviction/ fire built in you to cause you to shift out of park into drive?

_____

_____

If you haven't shifted into drive yet, why haven't you moved yet?

_____

_____

All movement isn't progress, so be sure you're moving forward!

CHAPTER 6

MOTION ISN'T PROGRESS
(RECOGNIZE WHERE YOU ARE)

Just like marriage, long-term career or job success isn't based on longevity alone. Just because you kept a job for 12 years does not mean you are successful in that role. Just because you've owned a business for 16 years does not mean you are successful. What if your business put you in debt and you had to work another job all 16 years just to break even, is that success? Working your business and another job to support your business – is that what you originally intended to do or want to be known by?

The two older couples challenged me to think about my marriage, my career, and my leadership ability. I have a couple questions for you that I asked myself:

1. Are you a Leader? A leader of what?

_____

_____

2. What evidence do you have to back up your claim of being a leader?

_____

_____

3. How effective are you in leading others? What ways have you measured your effectiveness?

_____

_____

4. Are you lucky or is there a set of behaviors you're practicing every day?

_____

_____

5. Are you fulfilled with what you're doing? Are you going through the motions every day or are you making forward progress? Explain your response.

_____

_____

Titles need leaders; leaders don't need a title! First, you have to recognize the greatness in you. It's the duty and obligation of your leaders/ mentors to draw it out of you. Naturally functioning at a high level and not pushing yourself or your teams to get better is "motion without progress."

Don't miss GREATNESS because you settled for what was good!

CHAPTER 7

THE ONLY COMPETITION IS YOU

As I started talking, I was in the conversation for about 30 minutes, then I realized, I'm having an "OLD" conversation in a "NEW" place.

What does the statement above mean to you?

_____

Service could be imparting some wisdom into someone without expecting anything in return, helping someone in your department by mentoring them, offering an encouraging word to someone who needs it, buying lunch for the person behind you in line, taking time to help a younger student in an area of your strength in school, serving the less fortunate, and many other actions. I have a few questions for you to consider:

1. What does it mean to you to serve?

_____

_____

2. What are you looking to gain in return from serving others?

_____

_____

3. Has someone served you?

_____

_____

4. How did that make you feel?

_____

_____

5. What is your response to someone else serving you?

_____

_____

I don't need to be associated with a particular group of people to define me. I'm not better or less than you. I'm me. You may not fit in with everyone or act like everyone, but that's okay. The exceptionally skilled individuals in life are those who are disciplined enough to work at being a better version of themselves. I have a few more questions for you.

1. Who are you living for?

_____

_____

2. What steps are you taking to become a better you?

_____

_____

3. In what ways are outside voices influencing your progress?

_____

_____

4. Who are you comparing your life to? Why?

_____

_____

5. Is your end goal to be the person you're comparing yourself?

_____

_____

Be you, and serve others by teaching them the same.

CHAPTER 8

THE STEPS

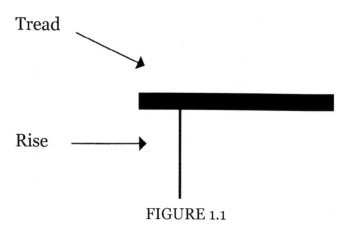

FIGURE 1.1

We need both parts of the stairs explained in figure 1.1, and we should live a balanced life of learning and application. I have a few questions for you.

1. What ways are you intentionally learning more?

_____

_____

2. What steps are you taking to apply what you've learned?

_____

_____

3. How will you teach what you've learned to someone else so they can start educating themselves and applying what they've learned?

_____

_____

4. Are you pacing yourself as you're taking the steps of life?

_____

_____

5. What clues have you identified within yourself that can help you as you're learning? (i.e. I need mini vacations/ staycations to keep me moving forward each quarter or awards and certificates motivate me to keep going once or twice a year).

_____

_____

As you walk the stairs of life, do not skip the application to gain knowledge only.

Don't stop learning!

CHAPTER 9

BIBLICAL PERSPECTIVE

Recently, I heard a college professor describe this faith race we're in like this, "Jesus ran the race, won it in record time; and, He takes the crown of victory off His head and places it on ours. Then Jesus tells us to take the victory lap. He says, 'I don't care how long it takes, if you fall or not, or if you stumble here and there. Just complete the victory lap.'"

For you to consider:

1. In what areas of your life are you celebrating God's victory?

_____

_____

2. What areas are you suffering defeat because you refuse to trust God in?

_____

_____

Oswald Chambers said, "The meaning of prayer is that we get hold of God, not of the answers."

One of the gentlemen I admired once told me, "If your home isn't ready for you to be promoted, you're not ready to be promoted." What a life changing statement! I can imagine many of you saying, "I'm ready to get promoted." It may require you to travel or relocate to another state.

1. You may be ready, but is your spouse ready?

_____

_____

2. You may be ready right now, but are your children ready to be without you an additional hour a day?

_____

_____

What have you learned or been challenged by in this chapter?
- Talking the talk, but not walking the walk
- Self-Examination
- The steps of a good man (woman)

_____

_____

CHAPTER 10

THE MENTAL CHALLENGES OF GROWTH

In Figure 2.1 we see a plant. You were probably raised and programmed to think like most of us - we're like a plant. We grow as children in an environment (dirt) where we're nurtured and educated (watered) by external resources. We have leaders and supporters (stem/roots) to influence us, and we bloom (flower) when all areas work together in concert. The result is the flower gets the opportunity to shine (get light) and help others grow (pollination).

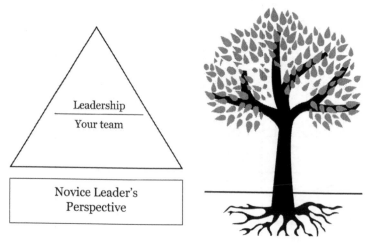

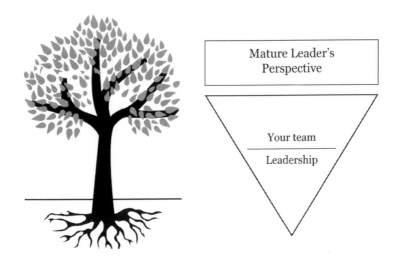

Figure 2.1

Candidly speaking, we should rally around our children like the process just described, and they will develop into beautiful flowers. When we're children, we're supposed to be that flower and get that light. When we start to understand the concept of leading ourselves, followership, leadership, parenting, and serving others, that same flower gets turned upside down. As a functioning leader, your responsibility is to become the stem/root so you can feed the people you serve (the flowers) what they need to grow and get as much light as possible. That means the functioning leader must transition from being in the spotlight (flower) to behind the scenes (stem/root) so others can grow.

How does FIGURE 2.1 and the concept around it speak to you and how you approach leading yourself and others?

_____

_____

_____

_____

CHAPTER 11

I GOT THIS!
(TITLE VS. FUNCTION)

Let's start this chapter with a few questions:

1. What kind of leader are you?

_____

_____

2. What behaviors do you exhibit consistently to back up your answer to question 1?

_____

_____

3. Would your spouse, parents, children, or closest friends say the same things about you as you've said about yourself in questions 1 and 2?

_____

_____

Experienced leaders have learned that the best leaders don't talk the most, they do the most.

People started viewing me as a high-functioning leader. My peers started to view me as the leader who cared, so I was sought out from the company and other businesses.

I have a few more questions for you:

1. Are you telling yourself that you're functioning in your role, or do you hear it from others?

_____

_____

2. What is your job description?

_____

_____

3. If you had to grade yourself in fulfilling your job description, what letter grade would you give yourself? A, B, or C?

_____

_____

4. What's preventing you from moving up to the next letter? Is it a skill issue or a will issue?

    a. Skill Issue: You need to be taught a skill to perform at a higher level. This is easy if there's someone to teach you and you're willing to learn and apply.

    b. Will Issue: You can fulfill the job description However, you WILL NOT because you don't want to.

_____

_____

5. Why should others follow you?

_____

_____

6. Who are you following?

_____

_____

CHAPTER 12

GOOD VS. GREAT

Your brand will be based on two major things, and we'll discuss them in more detail.

Mentality: Your perspective, how/why you think the way you do, and when you rest your brain.

Behaviors: What you do, how you do it, and when you do it. Behaviors also include your speech.

1. What do you see when you look in the mirror at yourself? Be as specific as you can.

_____

_____

2. Who built that image of yourself in your mind?

_____

_____

3. If you had to write your obituary, would it describe the person you are now or the person you want to be?

_____

_____

4. If you're not where you want to be, what's preventing you from being that person you want to be, NOW? (You may want to return to Chapters 2 and 3 to plan how to be that person you want to be. Many times, you need a mentor or coach to assist you.)

_____

_____

"Where the mind goes often enough, the body will soon follow."

CHAPTER 13

THE BUMP

Consider these questions for your Vision and Recovery:

1. What's your perspective before you get started?

_____

_____

2. How will you bounce back if something goes in a direction you weren't prepared for?

_____

_____

3. How will you recover your perspective?

_____

_____

4. How will you bounce back when you stumble mentally? When you're down in the dumps?

_____

_____

5. When you get frustrated with the process, how will you mentally pump yourself up?

_____

_____

6. What will your evaluation process look like? (If you don't have one continue reading.)

_____

_____

7. As a leader of people, how will you lead people and not projects?

_____

_____

8. What are your affirmation statements? Affirmation statements speak in present tense, not future tense.

_____

_____

You are great and are doing great things in life. You're changing your life and the life of others daily. Bounce back and lead on!

CHAPTER 14

BIBLICAL PERSPECTIVE

Whether or not you believe in Jesus as God, there's a truth here I want to share with you. You behave according to what you believe. Jesus believed he had to die for the sins of the world, so his actions accompanied his belief.

1. What do you believe at your core?

_____

_____

2. What's your purpose for waking up in the mornings? (It should be more than to make a dollar because that's vain.)

_____

_____

3. What are you making money for?

_____

_____

4. Do your actions line up with what you believe?

_____

_____

5. Do you have the perspective to back what you believe?

_____

_____

CHAPTER 15

QC SELF-EVALUATION

Allow me the opportunity of coaching you right now.

1. Concentrating on your end goal, are you committed to the goal?

_____

_____

2. What have you completed this month?

_____

_____

3. What did you do best to complete that task?

_____

_____

4. What can you do differently to complete the next task faster?

_____

_____

5. How did any distraction(s) take so much of your time?

_____

_____

6. What's the plan to prevent the distraction(s) moving forward?

_____

_____

I've learned to evaluate myself weekly. My end goal is to re-evaluate myself, daily, as my mentor is challenging me to do.

1. How often are you evaluating yourself?

_____

_____

2. Do you allow the people who follow you a chance to speak or make suggestions? If not, why?

_____

_____

I was better at consolidating my vision into one statement. Now I have a few questions for you:

1. How much time has elapsed since you revisited your original plan?

_____

_____

2. What has changed?

_____

_____

3. Is your vision changing? If so, explain how.

_____

_____

4. Who's influenced the change? How have they influenced the change?

_____

_____

5. Will you need to revisit Chapter 1 & 2?

_____

_____

6. Who's influencing your life and what do you have to show for that?

_____

_____

FINAL THOUGHTS

1. How has this resource benefited you?

_____

_____

2. Who will you recommend this resource to?

_____

_____

3. When will you recommend it?

_____

_____

As a part of the evaluation process I conduct on myself, I stop everything and listen to your feedback. Help me in this evaluation process by providing feedback about your experience with reading this book. Let me know if it was beneficial to you and how. Let me know if it wasn't beneficial at all. Your feedback is a part of how I evaluate myself and the material I use to coach others.

I want to leave you with my leadership statement: *"Worthwhile conversations will bring about worthwhile relationships. Worthwhile relationships will give you access. Access allows you influence."* - Nathaniel Woods Jr.

Lead on, starting with you!

Thank you for allowing me to serve you. If I or my team can serve you in a different capacity, please contact me at www.dotservice.org. Again, thank you!

ABOUT THE AUTHOR

Nathaniel Woods, also known to many as Nate, is the managing partner and co-founder of Developing Others Through Service, LLC (D.O.T.S). Before anything business, Nate is, first, a husband and father of two boys. Nate has had the privilege to be an executive advisor, coach, trainer, and keynote for many organizations, colleges, and universities across the world. He spends the majority of his time as the Professor/ Director of the Human Services program at Grays Harbor College in Aberdeen, Washington, and investing in real estate with Growth Vue Properties. Nate uses his business endeavors to fund humanitarian efforts of creating affordable housing, supplying clean drinking water in areas that are lacking, and doing missionary work.

Made in the USA
Monee, IL
16 September 2020